I0470315

People, Process, and Technology Management Framework

A Manager's Practical Guide to Establishing a Structure for Growth

By Kan Wang

ISBN-10: 1463617844
ISBN-13: 978-1463617844

CONTENTS

i

INTRODUCTION

Matt was clearly frustrated. What had begun as a simple request had quickly escalated into a frustrating question-and-answer session between him and his coworker sitting across the meeting table. As the company's production manager, Matt was always looking for ways to make his department run more efficiently. Early in his career, Matt was very hands-on and kept track of the entire operation. However, in the last few years, the company had experienced significant growth and upgraded its processes, which meant incorporating much more information technology. That, in turn, meant Matt had to ask the IT department for more and more help. Not only was it frustrating for Matt, who preferred to be self-sufficient, but after meetings like this one, it was maddening. From the other side of the table, Kyle, the IT manager, continued his list of seemingly endless questions.

"Okay, so you want to get production order information from the salespeople to your production schedulers sooner via a new application for your schedulers. My question is where that information is right now," Kyle said.

"It's in the company's existing application or databases. You should know – it was your department that gave sales their sales application to begin with," Matt shot back.

"We implemented a CRM for the sales department based on their requirements – that's got nothing to do with production."

Like I know what a CRM is, Matt thought. Out loud, he said, "Look, all I know is my production schedulers get a form emailed to them from a salesperson with a customer's order information and specs on it. But you know salespeople – sometimes it takes a couple of days for them to get around to it, and there's almost always some important information missing on the forms, which means my schedulers have to track it down before we can do anything with it. Those are days we could have the order to the customer sooner, instead of getting phone calls wanting to know when they're going to receive it. And sometimes they call before we've even received the order from sales! Do you know how stupid that makes this company look?"

Kyle said, "I understand the importance, Matt, but I can't just push a button and make it happen. I need some more information before my department can even begin to figure out what would be best. I mean, what specific data are you looking for? Does it have to be approved by the sales manager before it comes to your department? What are the parameters, criteria, and business rules for the flow of this information?"

"That's easy," Matt said. "Jack and Susan have been with us for years, so they know what they're doing – they don't need to pass their sales orders by Emily. Tom, on the other hand, is still pretty new, so I think Emily is still reviewing all of his sales orders first. As far as the data we need, the specs should all be in the form they email to us . . ."

2

As Matt continued, Kyle sighed inwardly. *Matt, for all of his competence, has absolutely no clue when it comes to IT*, he said to himself. Kyle faced the same challenge wherever he went. The company's managers knew IT is the future and that it would keep them competitive in the coming years – but they had limited knowledge of how to actually harness its potential. As such, Kyle spent part of his time trying to explain what IT could and couldn't do, part of his time creating a patchwork of applications to solve individual problems, and part of his time trying to keep it all working. He knows that creating yet another specialized application to handle another part of operations will ultimately create problems for Matt's department and his own in the future.

At the conclusion of the meeting, both managers walked out feeling they had accomplished nothing. Kyle had given Matt a list of questions he needed answers to before he could help; Kyle knew it was only a matter of time before upper management heard that Matt had found a way to shave a day or two off of order fulfillment and would tell Kyle to drop everything and make it happen.

For his part, Matt was angry that Kyle made it seem like such a monumental task to take a simple Microsoft Word document that the sales department *already had* and just speed up how soon his production planner got that information via an application to pull it from sales. *I mean, don't the sales people know that information as soon as they get the order from the customer?*, Matt thought.

The problem is not that either individual is incompetent or unmotivated. Both want to reach across the table and engage in a mutually-beneficial working relationship. And yet these two well-intentioned managers are about to spend thousands of dollars in application development, man-hours, training, and productivity, and cannot see a way around it.

There is a better way.

In a similar situation I experienced as an IT manager in a large organization, one of my colleagues summed it up perfectly. After some of our technical staff had created what she wanted and delivered it to her, she said, "Your department gave me exactly what I asked for – but not what I needed."

She was not the problem; she had a very clear idea of what she needed the technical solution to do. The problem was not the competence of the people in my department; after meeting with her, they delivered *exactly* what she asked for. The problem was that they were speaking different languages. She spoke in business terms, while the technical staff spoke in technical terms. If I had been present in the meeting, I could have interpreted between the two functional areas, but only because of my background in operations and IT management – a background most employees on either side do not have.

I have been on both sides of the table – as an IT manager like Kyle, administering IT resources, and as an operations manager like Matt, helping businesses reach the next level of operational effectiveness. I have worked with fledgling start-ups and with companies employing thousands of people, in industries as diverse as e-commerce, manufacturing, and government. My career spans from an in-the-trenches IT developer and tester at the bottom of the pyramid to a senior-level executive at the top of it. Even my education encompasses both business and IT with a master's in computer science and an MBA.

My experience has allowed me a unique perspective from both sides of the table and at both the bottom and the top of companies. In all that time, I have seen hundreds of scenarios similar to Matt and Kyle's played out.

Those experiences led me to develop the People, Process, and Technology Management Framework (*the PPT Framework*).

I designed the framework to help companies address the immediate challenges presented in the scenario between the two managers as well as some secondary- and/or long-term issues. The benefits of the management framework include:

- **Scalability:** able to be implemented at the company level, department level, or even functional level, while maintaining the ability to deal with various levels of complexity as the company grows

- **Knowledge management:** processes and procedures are documented and regularly updated, providing a valuable resource for each department and the company overall by removing the risk of critical knowledge residing solely in the minds of employees

- **Business continuity planning:** with documented operating procedures, operations become independent of key people or technology applications

- **Flexible structure:** a framework which lays the foundation to accommodate growth and the dynamics of the market while providing stability and structure

- **Increased communication and collaboration:** provides tools for inter- and intra-departmental communication, including setting mutual expectations and teamwork

- **Continuous process improvement:** by systematically organizing the elements of a business work system, the framework allows for quantifiable performance measures as each process can be systematically improved and optimized

- **IT-business alignment:** tools ensuring the alignment of strategy, processes, and technology in the short- and long-term
- **Business process management:** tools for documenting, organizing, and managing business work systems
- **Optimization of key performance indicators and metrics:** a systematic approach for breaking KPI determinants into their individual components and enhancing the effectiveness of each
- **Human interaction management:** a process-based approach for optimizing people's engagement with business work systems
- **Disaster planning/recovery:** inventorying business processes and IT solutions for disaster recovery planning

The PPT Framework is not designed to be an answer to all of a company's problems, nor is it designed to capture every single piece of data and information within a company's operations. Its purpose is to be a powerful methodology which provides a stable platform for managing growth and complexity, affording stability while also being flexible enough to allow for rapid operational change.

Similarly, this book's purpose is not to provide a step-by-step guide for implementing the PPT Framework for a specific industry, company, department, or process. It is a broad reference for those considering the need for the framework as well as those who are in the process of implementing it.

Implementing the PPT Framework never truly ends. As a business expands, as the market changes, as people come and go, and as new technologies are incorporated, a company continuously changes. Thus, this book addresses the specific elements of the framework – the building blocks, if you will – and provides an illustration of how it could be implemented by using Matt and Kyle's hypothetical situation.

While the company in the scenario is a mid-size company with a number of departments and managers, that does not mean the PPT Framework is only for mid-to-large organizations. Because of its scalability, the methodology is just as applicable for small businesses with only a handful of people. Because start-ups and small businesses often lack the resources to have specialized departments, many lack the structure and systemized approach of larger organizations.

As a small business grows, the principals of the company often do not have time to adequately train new hires and to communicate exactly how their company operates. The PPT Framework provides a key advantage by allowing the founders to document their priority processes, thereby shortening the time to train and communicate. For fast-growing companies, this is very important because some kind of structure *must* be implemented; waiting until a crisis point when structure is absolutely necessary will cost much more in time, capital, productivity, and other resources. By developing a systematic process while the company is small, the ideal structure will already be in place.

Larger organizations usually have processes and business rules. In this case, one of the primary benefits of the framework is allowing a standardized, company-wide system which incorporates existing processes while also allowing for much greater growth. More importantly, it provides a method of continuous process improvement towards optimal efficiency.

One of the appealing aspects of the PPT Framework is its simplicity. In fact, the whole framework can be summarized by a series of diagrams created by just two straightforward tasks:

1. *Inventorying the boxes* which represent the existing entities and the associated information for each one
2. *Drawing the lines* between the boxes which represent the relationships and flow of information between each entity

As an analogy to explain these two tasks: if I had just poured out a thousand-piece jigsaw puzzle of a mountain scene, at first I would have no idea how all the pieces fit together.[1] I would not solve the puzzle by picking up two pieces at a time to see if they fit together. I would look at the cover of the box and get the big picture – the snow-capped mountain, the green valley, and the blue sky.

If I were to apply the PPT Framework to the jigsaw puzzle, *inventorying the boxes* would be sorting and grouping the puzzle into distinct piles (which you could think of as invisible boxes). Blue pieces would go into the 'box' for sky pieces, white pieces would go into the box for mountain pieces, and green pieces would go into the box for valley pieces. After the initial sorting, I would sort the pieces further – perhaps separating the sky pieces into those with clouds and those without, or the valley pieces into those which were edge pieces and those which were not.

Drawing the lines would be seeing how the pieces fit together within their individual groupings. After fitting the pieces within each group together, I would see how each group fit with other groups, such as how the whole sky scene fits together with the whole mountain scene.

---

[1] This is exactly how many managers feel about their own department!

This analogy applies to every company, department, and existing process. The pieces of the puzzle already exist and, together, create the big picture. The manager's task is to categorize all of those pieces into distinct segments and then determine how each piece interlocks with the others.

Like the PPT Framework itself, this book is divided into five primary elements.

Chapter One: The Functional Organizational Chart captures the big picture of the company. It is not the traditional hierarchical chain-of-command type, but rather a representation of the high-level flow of information between company departments.

Chapter Two: Managing the People Component addresses the people element of the framework, separating individuals from their functional positions, and then matching those positions to processes.

Chapter Three: Managing the Process Component addresses how information flows through the company and how to separate the logical workflows from how the work is carried out physically (the standard operating procedures) – a crucial distinction within the PPT Framework.

Chapter Four: Managing the Technology Component addresses the role of information technology in facilitating people's engagement of the processes.

Chapter Five: Governance addresses how to maintain the PPT Framework in the long-term.

At its core, the PPT Framework is process-driven. While people may rapidly change, the functions required by a process remain more stable; therefore, the process determines the skills required in a position.

Technology rapidly changes, but the same information must pass from one position to another; while the technology may alter *how* people execute a process, the process still requires the same tasks to be performed.

It is difficult for me to stress the value companies can realize by applying the PPT Framework. The efficiency gains, the increased morale, the decreased communication problems, the cross-departmental collaboration – the list of benefits my clients and past employers have experienced goes on. But perhaps the most exciting idea is that the more they engage with the framework, the more benefits they will see.

If you are considering utilizing the framework for your own company or department, or even if you are in the process of doing so, I highly encourage you to continue down this path – for the sake of your company and your team.

I look forward to your success!

Kan Wang
June 2011

CHAPTER 1

THE FUNCTIONAL ORGANIZATIONAL CHART

While a traditional organizational chart (or simply, *org chart*) may represent the vertical chain-of-command and authority, it only captures a fraction of the true flow of information inside of a company. Most information and actual work flows horizontally (from one department to another), not vertically (up the layers of management). In fact, the only information which *should* flow up the pyramid are the reports required by each person's manager, new ideas, and a request for decision related to a process exception. In my experience with highly efficient organizations, only about 80% of operations are addressed by existing business work systems; about 20% of events are exceptions and require a judgment call on the part of functional staff. But only a fraction of those exceptions should require the input of a manager.

In other words, nearly all information and nearly all tasks are handled by functional staff members. Managers spend their time developing the functional staff's skills, validating the quality of work, optimizing processes within and related to their department, and addressing the process exceptions the functional staff request help on.

However, this is not the case in most companies.[2] Thinking of the company functioning as a pyramid lends itself to thinking of the company as individual "silos" in which departments are insular entities, developing their own culture, independent operating procedures, and even their own language.[3] Furthermore, many managers are so focused on addressing the problems their direct reports cannot handle that they are unaware of the root causes of those problems. By never creating a system to address the problems, they actually institutionalize the idea that any problem or exception to the norm should immediately be given to a manager to handle.

The PPT Framework provides a tool for examining the individual components of a problem, but begins with a top-down approach, starting with the functional org chart.

Although Kyle suspects Matt will escalate the production department's issue to senior-level management[4], Matt is reluctant to do so. Not only is Matt self-sufficient, he is also tired of having to involve the president every time he has an issue with IT. *There must be a better way*, he says to himself.

After searching online, Matt comes across *The People, Process, and Technology Management Framework*. Looking through it, he decides it might be just the thing he and Kyle could use to solve the problem on their own. While Kyle is initially surprised by Matt's suggestion, he readily agrees to try it. Like his colleague, Kyle is tired of unproductive meetings

---

[2] While there are companies or departments that come close to this ideal version of operations, most don't even resemble it.

[3] Which led to the problem of my technical staff creating exactly what my colleague asked for but not what she needed.

[4] See Introduction.

and running around in circles. If the PPT Framework can solve even a fraction of his problems with the production department, Kyle is all for it.

The two managers like the fact that the framework is scalable – that they can implement it just to address their immediate problem. The issue centers on the ability to move orders more quickly from the sales department through production to the warehouse in order to get them to customers sooner.

Matt's responsibility is the production department. His focus is on fulfilling work orders as efficiently as possible. In his mind, order fulfillment begins with an emailed form and ends when production hands the product off to the warehouse. But those two other departments are not Matt's concern. He answers to the president of the company for how quickly and error-free he fulfills customers' orders; anything beyond that is someone else's responsibility.

The two managers create a simplified org chart of the company, only including the departments related to their immediate issue. The org chart they create looks like Figure 1-1.

FIGURE 1-1

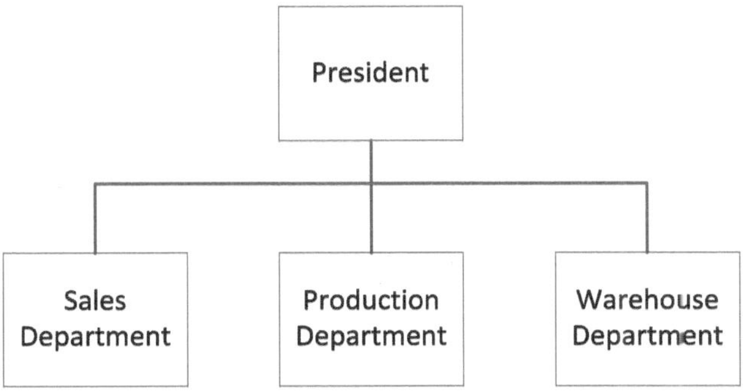

The reality is more complex, of course. The production department and the sales department are connected through a series of information flows back and forth. The problem is that while Matt instinctively knows about the interactions, he still has the mindset of a silo department manager.[5] When the IT manager, Kyle, asks him about how the sales department functions and how his department interacts with it, his instinctive answer is that that information is not his responsibility; besides, shouldn't IT have a better idea of how sales operates since IT set up the whole sales system?

On Kyle's part, he is frustrated because he believes a production manager should know everything about anything that comes in or goes out of his own department; after all, isn't that why Matt's salary is bigger than the IT manager's?

Again, the issue is not that either of these managers are incompetent or unmotivated. Matt is unable to peer into the inner workings of the sales department because, of course, that is not his department. Kyle, of course, only knows about the applications his IT department has put in place; how the sales department uses those IT applications is up to them.

Matt and Kyle could choose a haphazard approach, with Kyle talking to people in both the production and sales departments, developing some kind of working diagram of the flow of information, then conferring with his IT personnel to try to find a solution or build an specialized application to Matt's issue. However, the PPT Framework offers a more systematic approach, beginning with the org chart itself. In the place of a command structure, the PPT Framework focuses on the chart which:

- Defines departmental and functional boundaries
- Identifies the information flows between departments (i.e. *hand-offs*)

---

[5] Which can lead to turf wars, office politics, 'grenade lobbing', etc.

- Sets parameters for functional responsibilities
- Serves as a guide for decision making (i.e. the chain-of-command)
- Operates independently of the existing people in the company, focusing on function instead[6]

In the analogy of the jigsaw puzzle[7], the first step was to broadly group the different areas of the puzzle together. Similarly, with the PPT Framework, the first step is to group the broad functions of the company together. This is *inventorying the boxes* - creating boxes and placing the primary functions of the company in their respective boxes. While this may seem like an easy task, some people find it a challenge to think about the company conceptually instead of operationally. Since the PPT Framework is independent of existing people, the difficulty with most managers is in separating *how* or *who* performs the process from the process itself.

For example, if a small business was large enough to perform accounting and HR functions in-house, but too small to hire a full-time person for each, the company may hire one person to perform both roles.[8] In the company's functional organizational chart, however, there would be two separate boxes representing the two separate functions. This plays an especially important role in preparing for growth. When this hypothetical business grows large enough to hire a full-time HR manager, the functional org chart would remain the same because the *function* of HR would remain the same.

Once the broad functions of the company are in their respective boxes, the PPT Framework assigns each one a Department Title and a unique

---

[6] Some managers are more dominant and influential which often leads to them making decisions beyond their functional boundaries.
[7] See Introduction.
[8] Or combine IT and Operations, or Sales and Marketing, etc.

Department Identification Number (or simply, *Department ID*).[9] In regards to processes, the Department ID is the basis for the high-level identification of the origin and destination of information flows (the hand-offs) between departments, which lays the foundation for further identifying how each department actually interact with each other.

After Matt and Kyle create Department Titles and Department IDs, their diagram yields Figure 1-2.

FIGURE 1-2

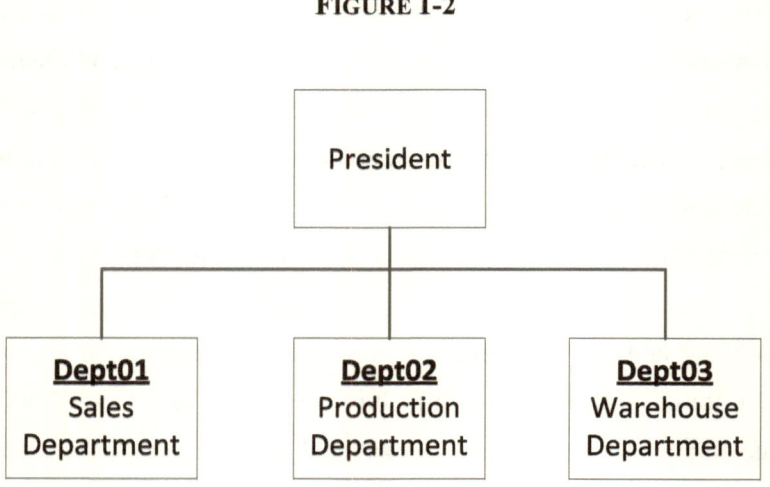

For simplicity's sake, this functional org chart looks almost identical to the traditional pyramid chart illustrated in Figure 1-1. However, a real-world application of the PPT Framework may result in an organizational chart which bears little resemblance to a company's existing one. How well-defined a company's functions are, how many people are filling different roles, how complex a company's operations are, how many layers

---

[9] You don't necessarily need to use the classification system in the book's scenario. The way you number departments, positions, IT applications, etc. should reflect the complexity of your own needs but, most importantly, be standardized throughout the company.

of functions there are[10], and other factors play a role in shaping the chart. After this, however, the similarities between the two end as the functional org chart becomes the basis for representing the dynamics within the company's work system.

After assigning Department Titles and Department IDs to the respective boxes representing a company's broad functions, the next step is to represent the relationships between the departments (i.e. *drawing the lines between the boxes*). These lines represent the hand-offs between departments – the information flows integral to a particular task.[11]

In Matt and Kyle's situation, the primary concern is getting the information from sales to production more quickly, allowing Matt to get the product to the warehouse more quickly. Thus, *drawing the lines* results in Figure 1-3.

FIGURE 1-3

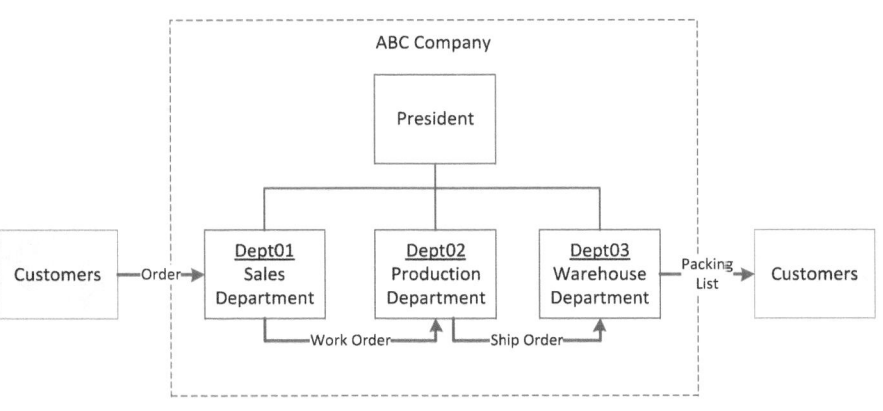

---

[10] For example, within the box representing production, you could break it down into production planning and the production line; how you apply the PPT Framework to your specific company, department, or function will be unique to your situation.

[11] It is impossible to capture every piece of information passed between two departments. Between emails, documents, calls, and one-on-one conversations, attempting to represent every possible interaction would be an overwhelming and, quite honestly, useless task. The PPT Framework is designed to represent the hand-offs critical to key processes. I recommend companies begin their engagement by identifying their critical success factors, such as order turnaround time, and trace how the hand-offs between (and within) departments affect those factors.

Now, Matt and Kyle's diagram represents the high-level process of how a customer's order is filled. Although this is a simple illustration, it is already a better model of how the company functionally operates than the pyramid chart in Figure 1-1 does. While there are far more hand-offs between these four boxes, Matt and Kyle stay focused on the immediate task at hand.[12]

Applying the PPT Framework is not a one-time project. Rather, it is an ever-expanding strategic initiative. At the beginning, the only elements of the company included in the framework are those departments and processes directly supporting a company's strategic objectives. As those elements are optimized and the overall structure of the framework set in place, the second tier of departments and processes supporting the strategic objectives can be incorporated. Ultimately, I advise companies that the goal is to capture about 80% of a company's critical operations within the framework.

In my experience, even for highly efficient companies, about 20% of all operations are unique events – exceptions to the norm, urgent problems, crises, etc. The PPT Framework is not designed to help companies completely eliminate problems, but to provide a structure for optimizing the recurring processes of the company. This, in turn, allows managers more time to adequately address the other problems and, hopefully, allow them to focus on the things which add more value to the company, such as crafting strategy, training, innovating, and other high value but low urgency type of activities.

In highly inefficient companies, however, I find the opposite situation where managers almost never have time for low-urgency activities because

---

[12] As you'll see, just 'zooming in' on Figure 1-3 will yield enough material for the rest of this book. Don't be intimidated, however; as you progress through the steps of applying the PPT Framework, you'll see how straightforward the process itself becomes, and how much time and effort the framework will save you going forward.

they always seem to be 'fighting fires' – quickly turning their attention from one problem to another. This crisis-of-the-day mentality is compounded by the fact that many managers are simply dousing the smoke and not addressing the true cause of the fire. Thus, the fire smolders in one area, only to flare up again in another. To the manager, it might seem like two separate occurrences; in reality, they may two symptoms of the same underlying problem.

Chapter Two: Managing the People Component addresses the idea that *people problems* are really *skill problems*, and provides managers tools for aligning people's skills with the needs of the processes they are executing.

CHAPTER 2

PEOPLE MANAGEMENT

While the human element was ignored in Chapter One, it is by no means ignored by the methodology altogether. People, in fact, are the most vital part of the framework. Processes cannot be performed and technology has no purpose without people to perform the work. The issue of managing people in general and the concept of leadership are beyond the scope of the PPT Framework. The people component focuses on aligning an individual's existing skill sets with a position's required skill sets, and the position's required skill sets are determined by the needs of the process(es) that the position is responsible and accountable for.

In other words, "people management" – for the purposes of the methodology – is actually the skill management of a person people filling a position. It has been my experience that many managers deal with symptoms of human resource problems (such as the action of an employee) instead of dealing with the source of the problem (such as the inability to perform a task). This is a sign that the manager cannot distinguish a problem caused by a person from a problem caused by the process itself.

For instance, the employee's action may stem from him trying to deal with an exception to the norm. If no clear business rule has been laid out guiding him on how to deal with process exceptions, then the problem may not be the employee but a lack of direction in performing the process.

However, when the right person is well-matched to a position, and the position is well-defined by the processes it is responsible for, a manager's problems with the person's performance goes down. Some people problems are actually inherent process or technology problems, and often it is a combination of the three. However, for problems which are truly an issue with a person, the focus – for the purposes of the PPT Framework – is not on the person but on the underlying skill deficiency needed for the position.

Soft skills deficiency. I have often seen the situation where a technical expert is promoted from a functional position to a managerial position based on their technical success. In their technical position, they needed a ratio of about 70% hard skills (i.e. the skills necessary to execute a process or task) to 30% soft skills (i.e. communicating, collaborating, decision-making, etc.), depending on the position; being in a functional position, they needed functional skills more. However, in their management position, the ratio is reversed; they need about 70% soft skills (to supervise others, deliver useable information to their superiors, collaborate with other managers, train their direct-reports, etc.) to 30% technical skills (so they can competently manage the functions for which they are responsible). But if they receive no training, it usually takes a long adjustment period for the technical person to adequately fulfill their managerial responsibilities.

Sometimes, it is not immediately apparent that a person lacks the soft skills for a job. I witnessed a situation in which a manager, after demonstrating his competence for a company's production process, was promoted to head of operations. He remained in the position for nearly ten years and became the go-to person for nearly every operational decision within the company. After a decade, however, the company owner realized the market had changed and tried to adapt with a substantial shift in operations. The operations manager was firmly entrenched in the management style and processes he had mastered over ten years' time and was a major obstacle to change. Eventually, he quit and the company lost an extremely valuable resource because he was not prepared to deal with *all* the responsibilities of his position, which included adapting to/managing change.

Hard skills deficiency. On the other side of the coin are incidents which reveal a lack of hard skills. While these include technical (functional) skills, they also includes a lack of training and experience. While many small businesses do not have the resources to provide training for their employees, many enterprise-size companies do not have adequate skill development processes in place, either. In the face of day-to-day operations and firefighting, many managers push individuals' development down on their list of priorities.

But by placing a secondary importance on their staff's skills, managers are trading one set of problems for another. The result is a team which does not possess the required tools to fulfill their responsibilities, resulting in them having to push their challenges across the department to a more experienced staff member or up the chain of command to the already-overwhelmed manager.

This creates a negative environment in which the few people who are able to handle the work are punished by being given more work, while managers are dealing with tasks that should have been handled by their direct reports.

The encouraging thing is that all of these issues can be addressed in a systematic way.

Just as the IT manager, Kyle, has been forced to solve company problems in a haphazard way, managers often approach people problems on a case-by-case basis instead of having a systematic process. By viewing people problems as skill deficiencies, the PPT Framework removes the personal element[13] and focuses on aligning skill sets with the process itself. Just as the methodology separates people from processes, it also separates people from their current position.

Most positions remain relatively stable compared to the person filling them. People may leave an organization, be promoted, be reassigned, etc., but the required tasks associated with that position still need to be performed. In separating the individual from their position, the PPT Framework minimizes the impact of staff turnover on the business.

Addressing the people component of the framework begins by examining the departments of the functional organizational chart and then determining what *functional positions* exist (or need to be created) to fulfill the broad functions of each department.

The Position Title and Position Title ID. The framework assigns each position a formal Position Title. Similar to a position job description, each title has a list of the skills required to perform the specific responsibilities of the position and, when possible, a quantifiable measure of each skill level.[14] Each title has a unique ID for easy reference.[15]

---

[13] That is, the framework attempts to make the process of managing people as objective as possible.

[14] This measure of skill level is important later in the section for managing the people-position distance.

[15] More than one person can have the same Position Title, such as three people all holding the position of Sales Representative. To standardize positions and language across departments, the framework requires the basic responsibilities of people holding the same titles to be identical. For instance, if a company has a position named Salesperson for both the corporate sales department and the retail sales department, the two positions would be very different in terms of function and scope of responsibility.

After Matt and Kyle assign Position Titles and IDs to the sales and production departments, their second diagram looks like this:

FIGURE 2-1

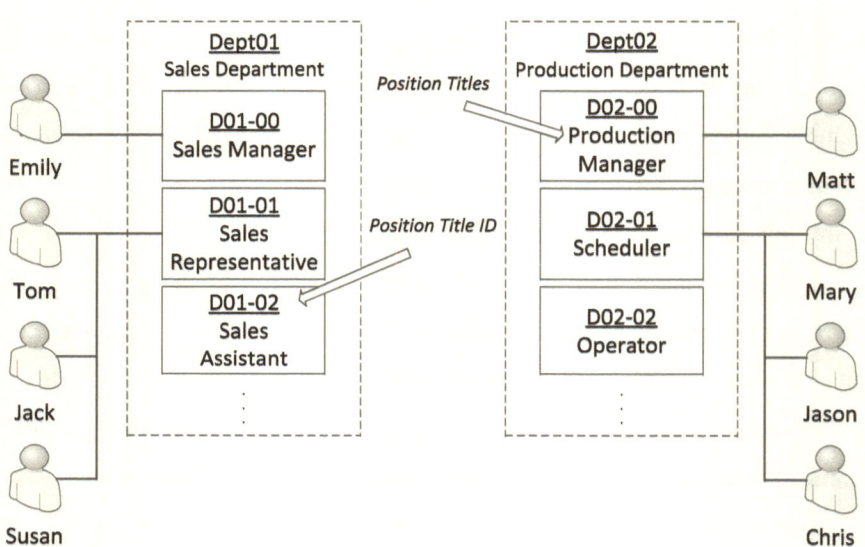

Tom is part of the sales department (Department 01), his formal title is Sales Representative, and the Sales Representative's Position Title ID is D01-01 (the Department ID plus an assigned number). Since Jack and Susan share the same Position Title, they share the same Position Title ID. The position and its ID remain constant, even if more sales reps are hired or if any of the current ones leave their positions. This also standardizes the job descriptions for the Position Title; regardless how many people occupy

---

In this case, I would recommend the company create a Corporate Sales position and a Retail Sales position in order to keep expectations, skill requirements, and terminology standard and to remove potential confusion.

the same title, they will all have the same requirements and performance expectations.

The Position Number. The Position Title has its own unique ID; however, there may be many positions which share a common Position Title (as with the sales reps); in this case, each position is assigned an individual Position Number. The importance of Position Numbers is they bridge the dynamic of employees changing, removing the uncertainty of people coming and leaving a certain Position Title. [16]

Since Matt believes the problem is in the sales department, they concentrate on assigning Position Numbers to the sales reps. They are now looking at Figure 2-2.

FIGURE 2-2

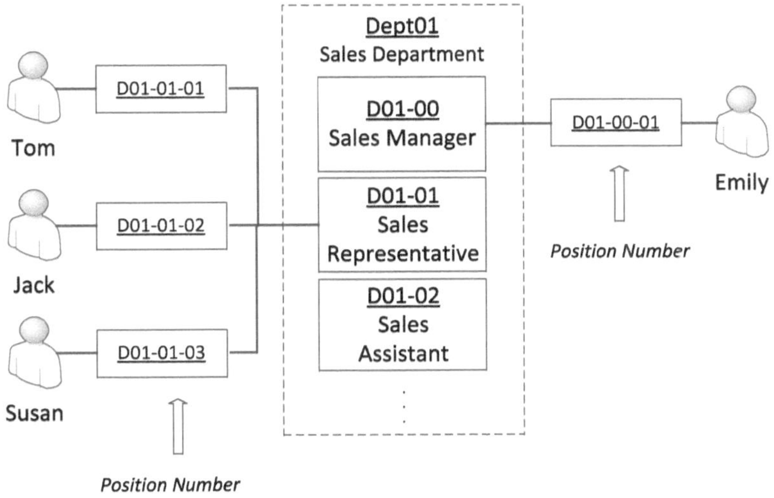

---

[16] As I said in a footnote in Chapter One, the classification system you use can be different than the examples provided here. In larger companies, HR may already have a numbering system for positions, people, etc. The most important idea is that these numbers should be standard across the company.

Position Title IDs and Position Numbers remain constant, regardless of whether someone is currently filling the position or not. For example, if ABC Company wanted to promote Tom (currently a Sales Representative) to Assistant Sales Manager, the company would first have to create and approve a new Assistant Sales Manager position with a new Position Title and Position Title ID. Tom's old position number (Position D01-01-01) would be vacant but continue to exist as an approved position to be backfilled through the hiring process. As long as the company did not eliminate Tom's old Position Number, the company would continue to budget for three Sales Representatives. Emily would have the authority to hire someone to fill Position D01-01-01 whenever she was ready.

In other words, an executive approved three Position Numbers for the Sales Representative Position Title, representing approval and budget allocation for three staff. Regardless of what Tom, Jack, and Susan do, Emily is approved for three Sales Representatives and can hire at-will.

By keeping people and their respective positions independent of each other, the framework provides a flexible platform which can easily accommodate such dynamics as employee addition and departure with minimum impact on the existing processes and ongoing operations in place. More importantly, it provides a model for financial and budgetary planning and projection for managers in terms of a department's labor costs.

The Employee ID. A Position Number stays with its assigned Position Title, regardless of employee changes; conversely, an Employee ID stays with an employee, regardless of that employee's position changes.[17] In the previous example with Tom, while Tom's position may change from Sales

---

[17] Some companies use an employee's Social Security number as their Employee ID, but I strongly advise against this. By assigning a unique Employee ID, the company can keep accurate records about an individual's employment without exposing the SS# outside of the HR department and put the personal information at risk.

Representative to Assistant Sales Manager, Tom's Employee ID would remain the same. This way, the company can easily keep accurate records about Tom by tracking his Employee ID with little impact from his changing job description, roles, and responsibilities associated with his new job title.

Linking Position Numbers. After Position Titles and Position Numbers have been established, creating the reporting structure is straightforward. With all the "boxes" of positions in place, Matt and Kyle simply draw the lines from each position to its respective manager. Each person has only one manager to whom they report, but a manager may have many people reporting to them. For just the sales department, Matt and Kyle have the following diagram:

FIGURE 2-3

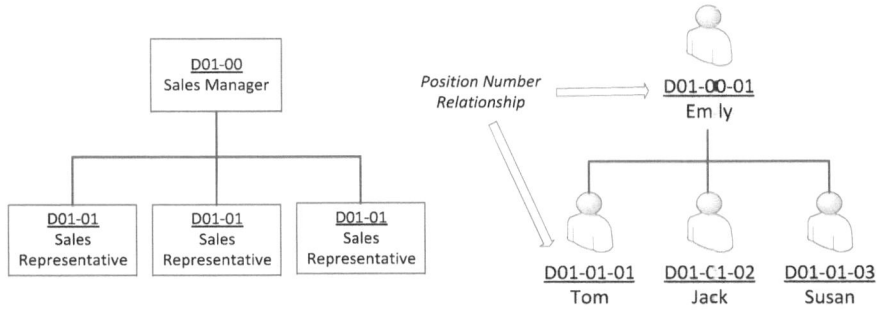

The Sales Manager (D01-00) supervises the position of Sales Representative (D01-01); currently, there are three Sales Representative positions approved by management. Furthermore, each position should link to one and only one department.[18]

It is important to note that in the Position Title diagram on the left, there are only two job descriptions defined for the D01-00 and D01-01 positions. In the employee diagram on the right, there are four people and therefore four distinct personnel HR records. Both diagrams indicate that Position Numbers D01-01-01, D01-01-02 and D01-01-03 all report to D01-00-01 – regardless *who* actually occupies any of the positions.

The main purpose for establishing a structure through unique identifiers for each Position Title, Position Number, and employee is to facilitate the 'moving parts' of these components as the company grows or changes, without jeopardizing the underlying management structure. Managing these relationships ensures the agility of the framework to account for changes in the dynamics of managing people.

After inventorying the boxes and identifying existing and/or needed positions within the functional organizational chart, the two managers' next step is to inventory each box with respect to the position's required skills. While Matt and Kyle do not have the authority to create an official job description for people in Emily's department, they can certainly do so for everyone in Matt's department.[19]

Crafting a job description which is well-aligned with the position and the position's tasks is one of the most important elements in not only the PPT Framework but in every business altogether. Without people who are

---

[18] This is true even when one person fills multiple positions, such as the example I provided earlier wherein someone was both the HR and Accounting Manager. In the PPT Framework, his Employee ID would link to two Position IDs. While not an ideal scenario, applying the framework to existing situations requires some flexibility. The most important thing to remember is that even a modified framework is better than no framework at all.

[19] Ideally, Position Titles, job descriptions, etc. are created in collaboration with the HR department. In Matt and Kyle's case, though, they are on their own.

able to perform their job, there is no one to execute the process and no need to use technology. Hiring someone who is unable to fulfill their responsibilities and who pushes everything across the department or up the chain-of-command may be worse for the operation than not hiring the person at all and distributing the responsibilities across the department anyway.

As addressed above, there are primarily two broad skill categories: hard skills, including functional skills and technical know-how; and soft skills, including the ability to work with teams, to effectively communicate, to collaborate, and to emotionally and mentally handle the job. The position's required skills and skill level should be completely independent of whoever is filling (or may fill) the position. In other words, if the perfect candidate could be found for the position based on the processes the position is responsible and accountable for, what would the person look like?

Hard skills are easier to quantify; soft skills, by their very nature, are subjective and therefore more difficult to objectively measure. Scholars debate whether someone can be trained soft skills – that soft skills are perhaps innate or can only be developed by the individual themself. Regardless of whether soft skills can be taught or not, every position in a company requires them to some degree.

'Managing the distance.' After defining the measurable and ideal skill sets of a position, the position's requirement can be compared against an individual's current skill set. Every manager wants an all-star team – people who are able to go above and beyond their position's requirements and responsibilities. The reality, of course, is this rarely happens. There is almost always a gap or distance between the existing skills of the individual and the ideal ones of the position. Figure 2-4 graphically illustrates this gap.

FIGURE 2-4

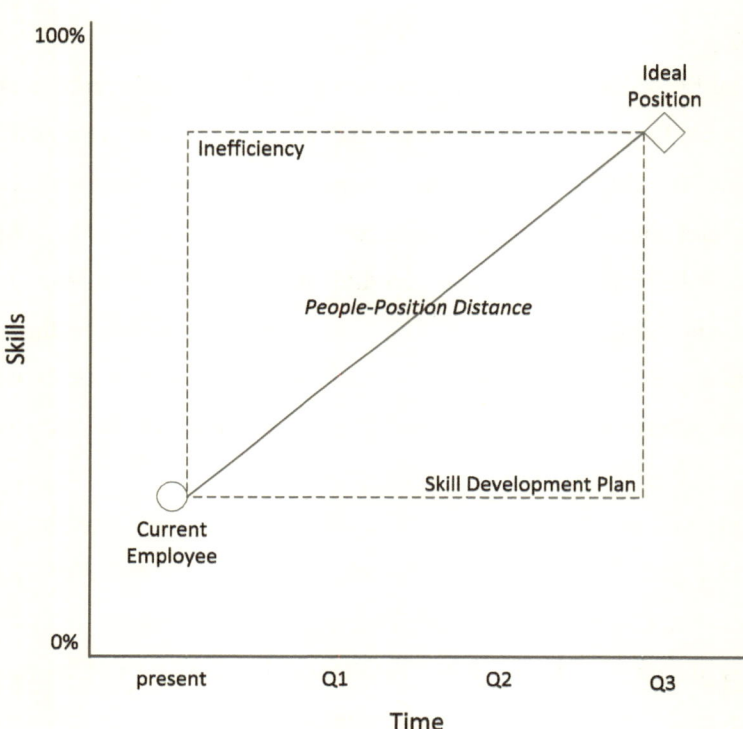

The distance between where the employee is and where they need to be has to be addressed in order to make the position (and the overall business) as efficient as possible. *Managing the people-position distance* is the process by which the manager provides resources and supports a person's development with a skill development plan.

There are a number of things to keep in mind in managing the people-position distance:

- The person may never reach 100% of the desired skill sets. However, the ideal position description establishes the ultimate goal and, by plotting the course between the current skill sets and that goal, the person has a clear direction and knows the expectation.

- The wider the gap, the longer it will take to address the deficiencies. It is the manager's responsibility to establish a set of acceptable parameters, including a timeframe for addressing deficiencies, providing adequate resources, and establishing clear milestones for the targeted level of improvement.

- A manager's assessment, skill development method, and time allocated to develop staff should be consistent across all staff.

Chapter Three outlines a method to continually improve individual tasks within each process in order to achieve maximum efficiency. Similarly, managing the people-position distance is the method by which an individual's skill sets are continually improved to continually stride towards maximum personal efficiency.

However, the biggest opportunity to better manage the distance is with new hires. By objectively comparing each candidate's skill sets against the quantified ideal skill sets of the position, a manager can save months (or even years) of skill development, as shown in Figure 2-5.

FIGURE 2-5

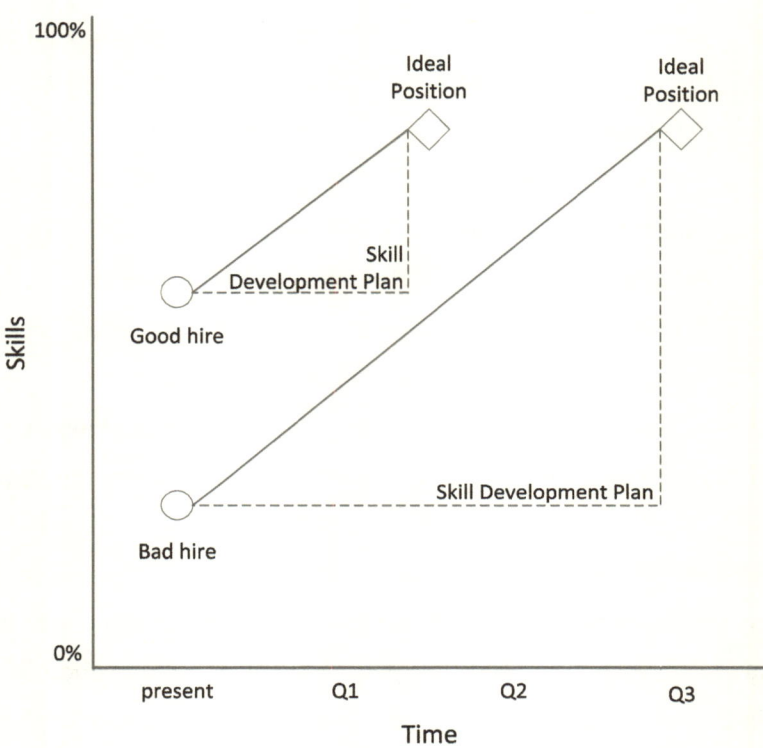

While hiring the more qualified candidate may seem intuitive, most companies do not objectively measure a candidate's level of ability in both hard and soft skills and then compare them to an objective measure of the open position. In fact, most interview processes are subjective, with interviewers looking over a resume and asking irrelevant questions – none of which may pertain to the position's requirements at all.

There are plenty of other good books from knowledgeable authors on how to prepare and conduct interviews. However, in the context of the PPT Framework, one of the most important points to remember is that managers hire *skill sets* suited to a position – not people suited for the manager's personality or a specific situation. A skill-centered interview begins by having a well-defined position description. This way, the candidate is judged against objective criteria with the goal of minimizing the people-position distance.

Having a well-defined position, with tasks and responsibilities clearly outlined, helps jumpstart the new hire and keep their morale high. As a personal example, I've worked for a number of employers and contract-clients who had no clear hiring process in place. My first day on the job, I was ready to give 110% in the exciting new opportunity. However, after a few weeks with no clear direction and trying to figure out the processes by myself, learn everyone's expectations of my position, making a lot of mistakes, asking 'stupid' questions, and generally at a loss, I was quickly demoralized. I felt unproductive and wondered if I was qualified for the position in the first place. While the methodology wasn't created for that specific situation, it certainly addresses the root of the problem: clearly communicating existing processes, assigning responsibilities, and setting performance expectations.

Business as a whole is more art than science; the goal of the PPT Framework is not to reduce the human element to a tool which executes a process. Rather, the aim is to help individuals find the position best suited for them and find individuals best suited for a position. With a person well-equipped for their responsibilities, their morale and productivity improves immeasurably, adding significantly to the business's bottom line. On the surface, the framework is about managing business work systems, but some of the greatest value it delivers is from the secondary products of applying the framework, such as higher morale and a better working environment.

In Chapter Three, the emphasis shifts from managing and optimizing the people component to the process component. In the spirit of standardization, many of the ideas from this chapter, such as assigning every identified entity a unique identifier, directly apply to managing processes as well.

CHAPTER 3

PROCESS MANAGEMENT

Process management is the core of the PPT Framework. The function of people and technology is to execute processes; the more aligned people and technology are to the processes, the more efficient the business will be (with the assumption that the process is well-thought out and fairly optimized). But the task of documenting processes is daunting for many managers. Where does one even begin?

A process is simply a sequence of tasks which is triggered by an event or incoming information, where the task is an action against the information which generates a desired output. In any business environment, it is the complex design and combination of processes that determine operational efficiency, productivity, quality, and – ultimately – the competitiveness of the business.

In the chapter on managing the people component, I addressed the issue that some people problems are, in fact, process problems. Here are more examples of process problems disguised as other problems:

- Managers who routinely spend a significant portion of their time firefighting, going from one crisis to another
- Functional staff who are unsure of what they can and cannot do, and so wind up doing nothing
- Functional staff routinely sending decisions to their managers that they should be able to address themselves
- Sending/receiving workflow items which are incorrect or which routinely have to be manipulated in order to be usable
- Inconsistent decision-making in similar situations
- Making exceptions to the standard operating procedure in the majority of cases
- Inaccurate and unreliable reports and data from subordinates
- Staff from one department unable to understand the workflow diagram from another department
- Unclear expectations between what is needed from others and what others need from the department (or staff)

Process improvement has been a buzz phrase in companies for many years. However, there are two major components which are crucial to process improvement but which are often overlooked by managers: setting a baseline (a starting point) to gauge progress, and then benchmarking processes against that baseline. There's not much value in trying to improve a process without having a way to measure the improvement. The key to process improvement is in optimizing incremental tasks within the process itself – not just gauging the final output of the system.

For example, in Matt and Kyle's scenario, Matt could perhaps convince the president that the sales department needs to hire a sales assistant to be responsible for the transfer the information from the sales representatives to Matt's schedulers; as long as the output of Matt's department justifies the expense, then the process has been improved, right? But is that really the best and most efficient way to reach the goal? Fortunately, Matt and Kyle are willing to dig a little deeper and look at all the moving parts of the system to figure that out.

As I related in the introduction, the methodology is not a one-time project – it is a process of continuous improvement, able to be implemented at any level. The starting point is identifying the critical success factors. In applying the framework to an entire company, this would be a business's core competitive strength and/or their strategic goals. On the level of an individual department, this may be the processes reflected in key performance indicators or the general measure of success the department manager provides to their higher-up.

The critical success factor Matt and Kyle identified was the company's ability to process sales orders more quickly in order to get the products to the warehouse (and therefore the customer) sooner. In creating the related functional org chart, they identified the departments to be included in the PPT Framework as sales, production, and the warehouse.[20]

In the diagram, Matt and Kyle identified that the broad steps of that process are:

1. Customer places sales order
2. Sales department submits work order to production
3. Production department makes product and notifies warehouse
4. Warehouse ships product to customer

---

[20] See Figure 1-3.

Of course the reality is more complex, but Matt and Kyle have identified the high-level hand-offs as an order goes from being sold to being shipped. In respect to the process management component, the rest of the PPT Framework consists of 'zooming in' on successive layers of these hand-offs to further define them.[21] To apply the PPT Framework to that process, Matt and Kyle have to identify the:

- Interdepartmental hand-offs – the information passed from one department to another
- Departmental processes – the broad steps of processing information and generating an output
- How to execute a step process – within a department's process, the step-by-step tasks of carrying out a process
- Standard operating procedure – *how* each task is physically accomplished (i.e. the technology used)

In Matt and Kyle's situation, they have already identified the interdepartmental hand-offs: the work order and the shipping order. Next, they assign a Departmental Hand-off Agreement ID (or simply Agreement ID) to these two high-level information flows. The Agreement ID begins with the Department ID which originates the information, then the Department ID of the destination department, and then a number specifying the specific document. While this sounds complicated to the two managers at first, they see it is fairly straightforward after adding it to their existing diagram, shown in Figure 3-1.

---

[21] Again, the entire PPT Framework is captured in just two tasks: inventorying the boxes and drawing the lines.

FIGURE 3-1

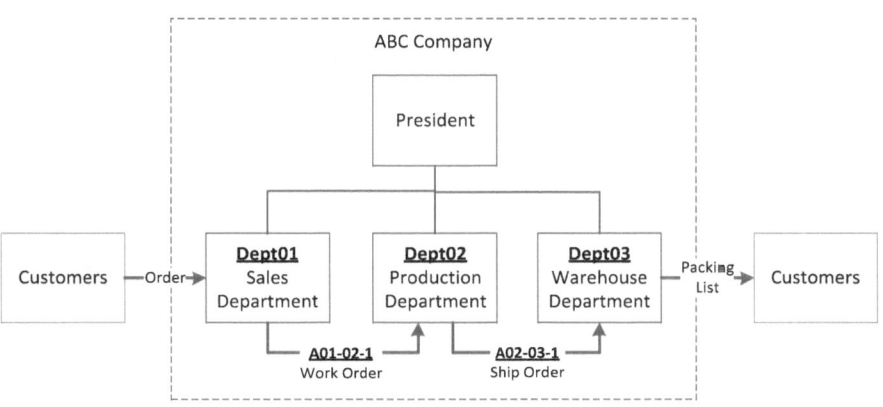

Matt and Kyle have designated the sales order as A01-02-1. 'A' signifies it is an agreement, 01 signifies it originated from Department 01 (the sales department), -02 signifies the information is being passed to Department 02 (the production department), and the final -1 because it is the first agreement identified between these two departments. (In the future, the managers may want to expand the PPT Framework to include other processes.)

Similarly, the shipping order sent from production to the warehouse is A02-03-1: the agreement is sent from Dept02 to Dept03, and assigned -1 because it is first agreement identified between production and the warehouse.

Matt and Kyle know there are far more interactions between all three departments, but their focus remains cutting down the time it takes the sales department to send production a work order. Later, as they expand the PPT Framework to include other important information flows, their diagram may look like Figure 3-2.

FIGURE 3-2

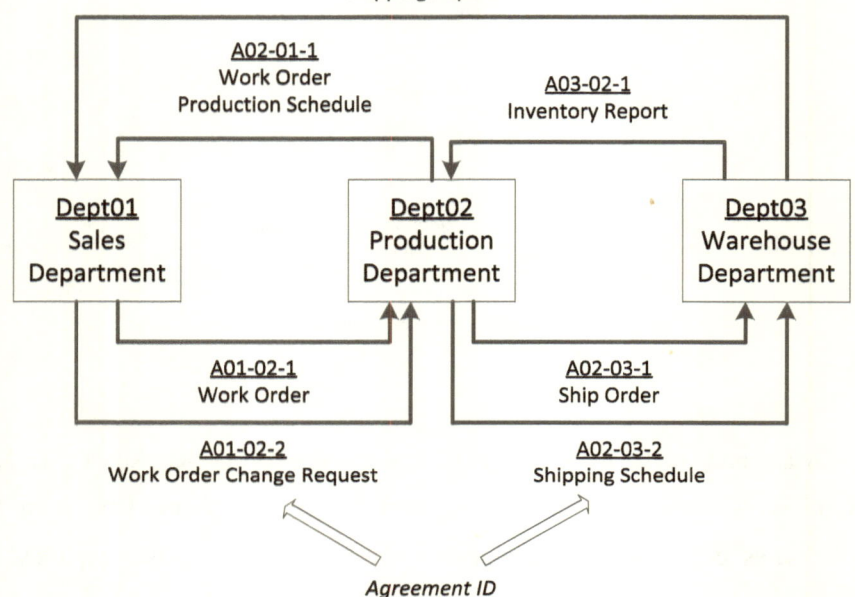

Agreement ID

The Agreement ID refers to the hand-off of information, like a form or email. However, the Agreement must have an associated document on record explicitly stating what information – exactly – must be provided each time there is a hand-off. The document must be solidified and agreed on by each manager in order to standardize the information flows between the departments. At the Agreement identification level, this is an agreement between two department heads. However, due to the political issues often present in many companies, many of these hand-offs are left unstructured and undefined. Managers unwilling to work with each other to reach an agreement will result in leaving the fight for the staff of the two departments to deal with. This fosters negative culture and enforces silo and turf wars. It is my opinion that this negotiation of the structured hand-off agreement should be dealt with by the managers, regardless how ugly the negotiation may be. It should be conducted behind closed doors at the managers' level until it is resolved.

By implementing a systematic approach at the beginning, Matt and Kyle (and whoever else in the company eventually uses the PPT Framework) can easily inventory and keep track of the boxes and the lines (hand-offs) linking the boxes.[22] Armed with their diagram, Matt and Kyle approach Emily (the sales manager) with a list of the information Matt's production schedulers need for each work order (A01-02-1).

After reviewing the list, Emily points out that, while she would be happy to help in whatever way she can, if the production schedulers had access to the sales application, they could get all the information they needed for themselves *without* having to wait on a sales rep to do it for them.

As it is, her sale reps constantly complain to her that they do not have time to come back to the office to email every information request from the production department; all the information production needs is in the sales department's CRM. Furthermore, Emily informs them, the customer specifications are almost always the same for repeat customers which account for 80% of the sales; her sales reps resent having to email the same specs every time an existing customer places an order.

However, Emily does acknowledge that on some occasions, her sales reps fail to obtain all the necessary specs, particularly with new customers. When this happens, it's not until the production schedulers bring the missing information to Emily's attention that she goes through the effort of contacting the new customer, getting the missing information, and relaying

---

[22] As I said in the introduction, the PPT Framework addresses not only immediate problems, like Matt and Kyle's example, but long-term problems, like improving other critical workflows in the future. With a framework already in place, it becomes much easier to systematically approach other issues going forward.

it to the production department, altogether delaying the production schedule by many days. Emily realizes that her sales reps could speed the process along by being more thorough with new customers.

Together, Matt and Emily create an Agreement document (A01-02-1) stating the information the CRM needs to have before creating the work order. Knowing the criteria which *must* be part of the work order, Kyle can configure the CRM to alert the sales rep when the information is missing and won't allow them to send on a work order until they enter it.

But the main issue, Matt realizes, is not with sales but within his own department. Fortunately, Kyle assures Matt that giving his production schedulers restricted access to the sales application is easy, and training them should not take long.

At this point, Matt already sees the benefit of the PPT Framework. Using the tools within the framework, Matt began a conversation resulting in the resolution of a long-standing conflict between his and Emily's departments, leading to an effective way to increase both departments' efficiencies.

After identifying the Departmental Agreement Hand-offs and reaching an agreement with other departments, the next level of process management is to examine the inner workings of a department's process. Matt and Kyle had been prepared to examine the sale department's operations, but after speaking with Emily, they now realize they should begin with the production department.

Since Matt knows his department well, he is able to quickly identify the four processes that convert a work order (the department's input) into a shipping order (the department's output):

1. Validate the work order

2. Check material inventory

3. Schedule production

4. Run production

To help Kyle understand, Matt draws the boxes representing the four processes and the lines as information flows from one box to another. Figure 3-3 is simply Figure 3-2, but zoomed in on Matt's department. Just as they did in Chapter Two, Matt and Kyle assign a name and ID to each box of their diagram.

FIGURE 3-3

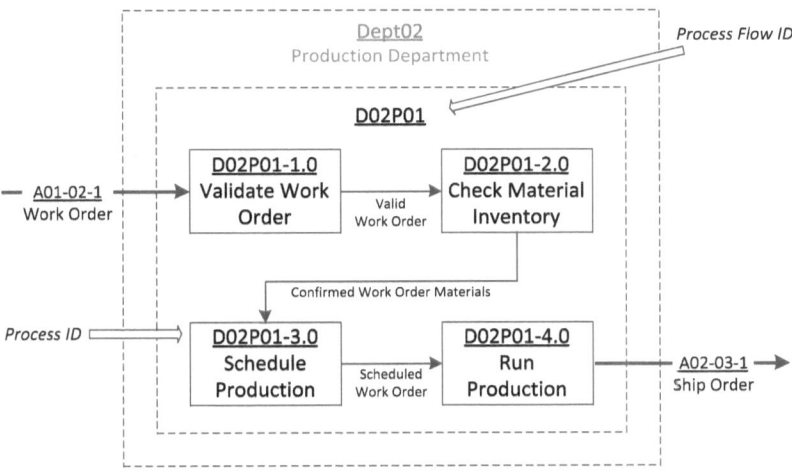

In Figure 3-3, an incoming Work Order Agreement triggers a series of four processes (collectively referred to as a *Process Flow*); the output of this Process Flow is a Ship Order Agreement, notifying the warehouse that an order is ready to be shipped to the customer. The PPT Framework breaks every entity (be it a position, department, or process) into its component parts and then assigns an identifier for each component. Thus, there is a Process Flow ID and then a Process ID for each of the processes within it.

Process Flow ID. In the case of Matt's department, the collection of processes related to fulfilling a work order is assigned Process Flow ID D02P01; D02 to reference the department (Dept02) and then P01 because it was the first Process Flow identified within the department.

Process ID. After identifying the collection of processes, the next layer of granularity in the framework is to assign each individual process its own ID. Matt identified the four general processes that have to be accomplished in fulfilling a work order. Each Process ID begins with its respective Process Flow ID – in this case, D02P01 – plus an assigned number representing its sequence. Thus, D02P01-1.0 for the first process (*Validate Work Order*); D02P01-2.0 for the second process (*Check Material Inventory*); etc.

As Emily pointed out, the bottleneck in Matt's department is in having access to all of the order specifications needed for the production run. Accordingly, Matt and Kyle focus their efforts on D02P01-1.0 – the process of validating the work order for completeness and accuracy.

Work Task ID. Each of Matt's four processes is further broken down into individual work tasks; those work tasks take their IDs from the already-created Process ID. Matt identifies four tasks within the Work Order Validation Process (Process D02P01-1.0), as shown in Figure 3-4.

FIGURE 3-4

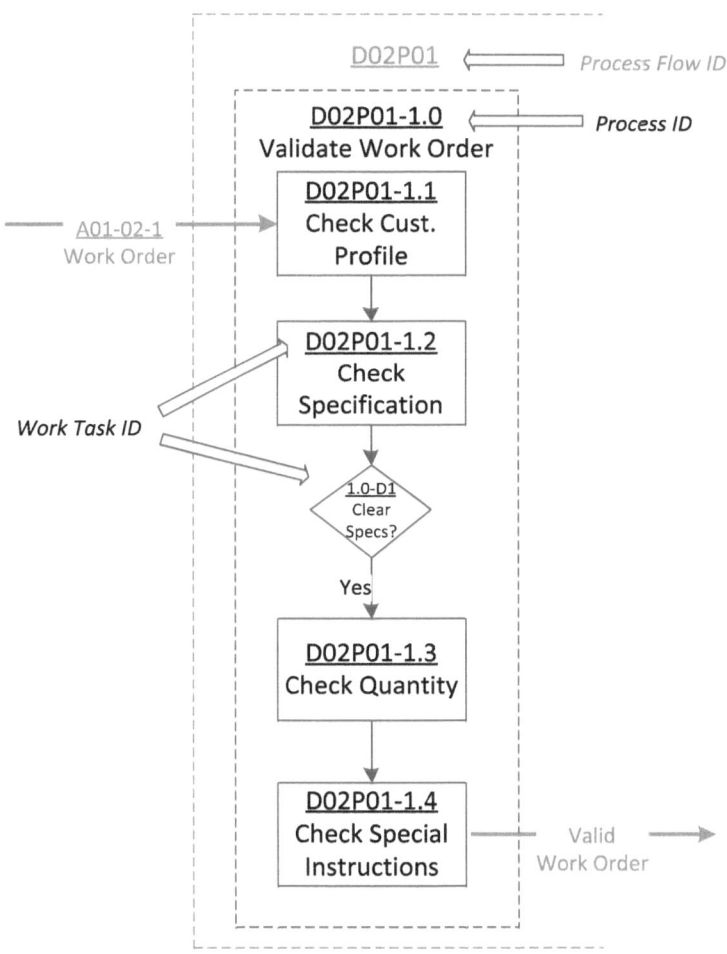

Figure 3-4 is simply Figure 3-3, but zoomed in on the Validate Work Order process box. The Process ID for the Validate Work Order process is identified as D02P01-1.0; the Work Task ID for each task within that process is assigned a sequential number: D02P01-1.1 for the first task in the process (*Check Customer Profile*), D02P01-1.2 for the second task in the process (*Check Specification*); etc.

It is important to note that even at this level of granularity, Matt has not specified exactly *how* each task is accomplished – only that certain tasks have to be performed. By separating *what* needs to be done from *how* it needs to be done, the PPT Framework offers a high degree of flexibility.

The current way to check the specifications of a work order involves the production schedulers pulling the information from the sales representatives' emails. Matt and Kyle know that they will shortly change the *way* the specifications are checked. However, by separating the process tasks from how the tasks are carried out, Matt and Kyle will not have to change their workflow diagram once they train the schedulers how to access the sales CRM. All they will need to change is the document explaining *how* and *where* the schedulers check a work order's specifications.

After Matt applies the PPT Framework to his department's main Process Flow, Kyle understands how work orders are transformed into production. Although Kyle was peripherally aware of the department's operations, having the process laid out in a task-by-task sequence helps him clearly understand the problem he and Matt are dealing with. More importantly, Kyle is recognizing how information technology can be aligned to business to facilitate and enhance operational goals and objectives.

Linking Position IDs and Work Task IDs. Once Kyle understood how information flowed through Matt's department, he realizes that if just the person(s) responsible for D02P01-1.2 (Check Specifications) had access to the sales department's application, the entire issue might be resolved; no one else in the department needs access to the CRM. For Matt, this would mean not having to train the entire department on using the sales system, saving him time, money, and productivity.

Further, with a full understanding of the processes, Kyle saw that instead of waiting for sales to confirm that all the work order information is complete and ready for production, IT could configure the CRM to automatically alert production that a work order's data is complete and ready for production (based on the criteria agreed to in the Work Order Agreement). This would further decrease the lag time between the sales and production departments.

Matt and Kyle's next step in applying the PPT Framework is to link each task with the position(s) responsible for carrying it out. While all of the people involved in the process of validating a work order are production schedulers, different schedulers are responsible for different tasks. In order to identify who *exactly* needs access to the sales application, the two managers need to assign each task to the position(s)[23] that carry it out. Working together, they produce Figure 3-5.

---

[23] It is important to recall the distinction between positions and people; while people may come and go, the responsibility of executing a task will remain with the position.

FIGURE 3-5

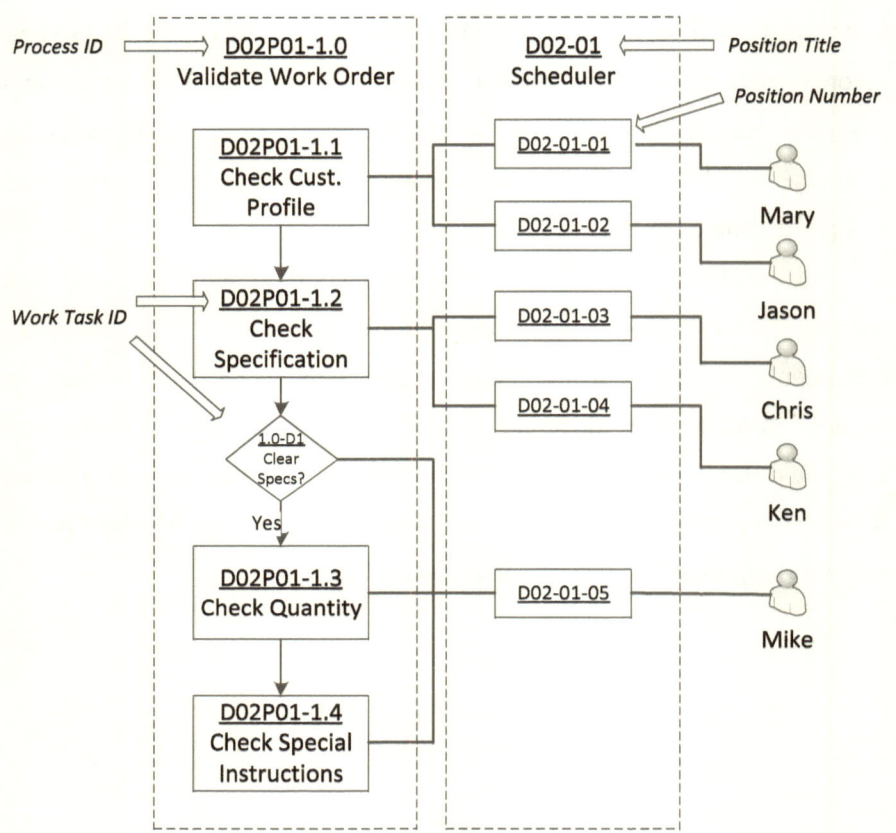

By linking Position Numbers to Work Task IDs, Matt and Kyle have identified that Chris and Ken are the two schedulers responsible for checking work order specifications. Therefore, in order to address Matt's issue of speeding up production, Positions D02-01-03 and D02-01-04 need access to the sales department's database so they can see all the work order specifications for each customer.

Currently, that means Chris and Ken need to be trained on how use the sales department's database. Going forward, however, Matt now knows that *whoever* fills those two positions needs to be trained as well. Accordingly, Matt updates the job descriptions for Positions D02-01-03 and D02-01-04.

Standard Operating Procedures. At this point, Matt and Kyle have a clear idea of how work task D02P01-1.2 should be performed and they have enough information to start writing standard operation procedures (or simply, *SOPs*).

The SOP is a document which specifies exactly how a task is executed – the IT applications, the judgment criteria, the business rules, operating parameters, exception handling, etc. The identifier assigned to each SOP is exactly the SOP's respective Work Task ID, as shown in Figure 3-6.

FIGURE 3-6

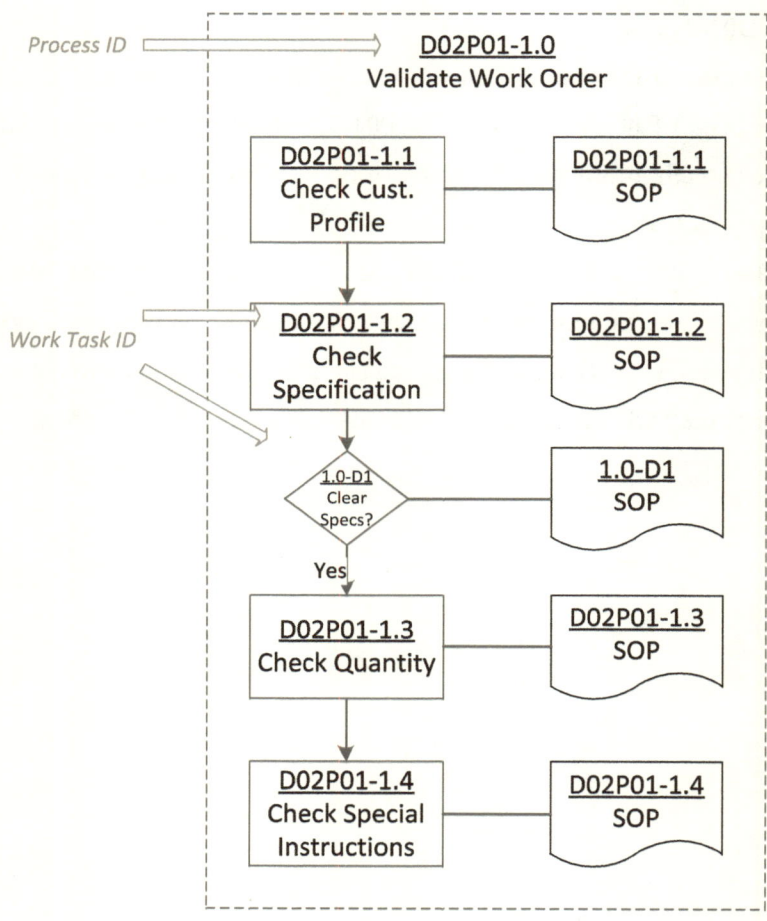

Each Work Task ID box from Figure 3-4 will have an SOP developed to explain how to carry out the process. In general, the format of the SOP will depend on the company, complexity, and/or the tool. If the process is fairly straightforward and relates to a very functional task, a descriptive format outlined in steps (*Step 1:..., Step 2:..., etc.*) may be sufficient. If the process is more complex and requires a certain level of expertise to avoid mistakes/exceptions, then a detailed physical work flow diagram in addition to a descriptive procedure may be helpful. Lastly, for businesses with a wider adoption of information systems that automate many of the work tasks through multiple systems, then the use of screen illustrations along with descriptive information may be the best choice. The bottom line is that at the SOP level, it is really whatever format will work that will best provide staff with clear instructions to consistently carry out the same task efficiently and accurately, and at the same time allowing for a document format (used to capture the instructions) that is easy to maintain and is consistent across the company.

As I pointed out in the last chapter, many of the benefits of the PPT Framework are not immediately apparent. Using the ongoing scenario to point out one of these benefits: Matt's knowledge is a valuable resource to the company, and if Matt suddenly left the company for whatever reason, it would take months for Matt's replacement to learn how the production department operates. With documented processes and SOPs in place, Matt's replacement could learn in a matter of minutes what might otherwise take days of observing and questioning.

Another benefit is that Matt now has the ability to measure and compare the individual performances of Chris and Ken, the two schedulers responsible for checking order specifications. By measuring the time from when each person received a notification from the CRM to the time Ken or Chris cleared the order and entered it in the production schedule, Matt can compare how long (on average) it takes each scheduler to perform a task. Furthermore, Matt not only can compare performance but can measure the affects of incremental tweaks to the system. In other words, he can endlessly optimize all of tasks leading up to this one to see how it impacts Chris and Ken's performance until each of them reach their full potential.

Four layers of Titles, IDs, and documents sound like a lot, but there is a very good reason for it. In designing the PPT Framework, I wanted to provide my clients a tool that would allow for a solid organizational structure with enough flexibility that their company would not be restricted by internal dynamics or market changes. Instituting successive layers of process detail provides the ability to change targeted aspects of a department's operations – such as switching to a different email provider or updating the decision-making criteria for a specific task – without having to change everything before and after it.

More importantly, the framework provides information and visibility for decision-making to assess impact when considering change in any part of the process before actually committing to the change. It provides managers a proactive method of improving processes, moving away from the trial-and-error approach.

It would be like if you had a storage room for all of your paper files. As you accumulated more boxes of files, you could simply stack all the boxes on top of each other. But if you later needed a particular piece of paper in a certain box at the bottom of the stack, you would have to unstack all the boxes on top of it in order to reach it. If you would install shelves in the storage room and then stack all of your file boxes one-deep on each shelf, it would be very fast to pull a particular file. And if you provide an ID method for the shelves and boxes, you could add or remove papers at will without compromising the order of any other papers or boxes. Implementing these successive layers of granularity allows for a high degree of flexibility while at the same time remaining very structured.

Additionally, tackling each of those layers from the top down is much more efficient than looking at the ground-floor activities and trying to piece a process together. Beginning with the broad agreement between departments and then zooming in on each layer of granularity allows a manager to effectively address the major elements of each layer and then refine the focus on the smaller components within each one.

By inventorying the boxes and drawing the lines, Matt and Kyle have determined the solution to Matt's original problem is much simpler than they both originally imagined. Additionally, by defining and committing to the hand-off agreement with Emily, Matt has mitigated further miscommunication between the two departments. Giving two production schedulers access to the sales department's application will:

- Cut down order fulfillment time by one to two days, making the customer happy
- Solve Matt's problem and make his department look better, thereby making Matt happy
- Remove the need for the production schedulers having to wait on return emails from the sales department, making the schedulers happy
- Remove the need for the production schedulers to email the sales department at all, making the sales reps happy
- Remove the need for Kyle to develop a custom solution and support yet another application, making Kyle happy

Having addressed the functional org chart, the people component, and the process component, Matt and Kyle turn their attention to the technology component in Chapter Four.

CHAPTER 4

TECHNOLOGY MANAGEMENT

Michelangelo is considered one of the greatest artists in history; Shakespeare, one of the greatest playwrights; Beethoven, one of the greatest musicians. Compared to modern technology, their tools were primitive. But even with all of our advances, few people today can achieve even a fraction of what these masters did. The moral of this example is that technology does not create, innovate, or deliver anything; it's still up to people.

When it comes to performing work tasks in a business, it does not matter how powerful the technology is – if users are unable or unwilling to use it, or if the process it is trying to automate is ill-defined to begin with, having access to powerful technology will not address the real problem or achieve goals. One of my colleagues summed it up well when she said that if a manager creates a bad process, IT will simply automate a bad process.

As someone with an IT development and IT management background, I know firsthand how rapidly the field changes and how overwhelming trying to keep up with those changes can be. It is even more frustrating for people who entered college or the workforce before I did because they may not have had much (if any) IT training, as IT is still a relatively young industry.

On one side of the table, people hope technology is the silver bullet – a magic solution which can address all their people and process problems. On the other side are those who aren't quite sure what the full capabilities of IT are, and so never take full advantage of it. Using technology to address a person's skill deficiency, to automate a process which has no standard, or to generate reports based on bad data will almost inevitably lead to "technology problems."

I designed the technology component of the PPT Framework around the idea that non-IT managers should be able to easily communicate with IT staff without needing to speak the language of computers. Likewise, IT managers should be able to communicate with their counterparts throughout the company without having to translate it all into business.

Another focus of the methodology was that IT should not play the central role in a business; processes and the people performing them are the most important element in an organization, and technology is simply a tool for people to execute those processes more efficiently and effectively. As I pointed out in Chapter Three, I believe only about 80% of a business's total operations can be governed within business rules and preset parameters. The other 20% fall outside of normal operations and must be addressed using judgment, additional skills, or analysis – and those actions require human input. Even more importantly, technology should *enhance* processes and people's abilities, not limit them.

Here is personal example of exactly what I am referring to. My wife purchased a jacket from a department store during a $10 discount promotion. A few days later she was shopping at the same department store at another mall and spotted the same jacket for $20 off. Still in possession of her receipt, she approached customer service and asked for the $10 difference, perhaps in store credit or on a gift card. The representative informed her that the store's system did not allow that type of transaction. My wife pointed out it would be the exact same thing if she would just bring the jacket in for a full refund and then made a new purchase.

The point of the story is that a customer should not have to come up with creative ways to circumvent an IT system, and that an employee should not be forced to think in terms of what the IT system will or will not allow when conducting business. This is a real-world example of how businesses (and customers) are being forced to operate around IT instead of IT being designed around people and processes.

In the 1970s, the positions of developers, programmers, business system analysts, or anything of their kind in the business world were nearly non-existent. Businesses were run and processes were designed by managers who were intimately familiar with their own departments and knew how they functioned.

Today, nothing has changed. Business managers *still* need to know how information flows through their department, even if much of it is handled by technology. Even if they do not completely understand how a technical solution functions, they should still know the tasks that need to be performed. Managers in the corporate environment deal with information (data) entry, storage, tracking, access, changes, approval, and presentation (reports). Prior to IT, these were managed with paper, business stamps, file cabinets, and typewriters. Today, the change in the medium does not mean the IT staff should take over the decisions and responsibilities of how a department operates; IT should only facilitate a manager's processes with newer tools.

Another of the PPT Framework's benefits is that it allows functional managers to design their department's processes *without* having to be an expert in IT. I have witnessed business managers who relinquished the operational decisions of their department over to a technical solution provider because of the application the provider installed. Thereafter, when the application changed, the department had to update their process to align with the application. This is the complete opposite of how departments *should* run – applications should change to reflect changes in the process.

An operations manager who has bad information and metrics by which to make decisions will likely result in bad decisions; bad information or incomplete requirements given to IT staff will result in a technical solution more limiting than one which increases efficiency and productivity.

On the other hand, there are departments who approach technology haphazardly or as a solution to a bigger problem. For example, a manager complained one of his direct reports was always late to meetings and wanted to design a reminder feature into the company's core operation application. While the company's IT department could develop the feature, the real problem was that the direct report lacked the soft skill of punctuality – and all the technical solutions in the world would not be able to change that.

Fortunately for our hypothetical example, neither Matt nor Kyle are of those mindsets. They both believe that processes are central to a successful business, that positions well-aligned with executing those processes are critical, that the people well-trained for their respective positions are crucial, and that technology is simply one of many tools to use in their position.

Applications. Matt and Kyle have determined the potential solution to Matt's problem is to grant access to the sales department's application for two of the production scheduler positions (the two currently occupied by Chris and Ken). In Chapter Four, they began updating the related SOP, but since the SOP specifically references an IT application, they have to first take inventory of the production department's IT applications.

For the purposes of the PPT Framework, *technology* refers specifically to information technology. *Application* refers not only individual programs (such as Microsoft Outlook or a company's customer database) but any IT resource which facilitates process execution. For instance, if a single Excel spreadsheet has a company's entire production schedule on it, then the spreadsheet file itself should be considered an IT application; if there are multiple Excel sheets for different operational purposes, they are treated as multiple applications.

With Kyle, Matt inventories all the IT applications his department uses on a regular basis and comes up with five, plus the sales department's customer application they need to begin using:

1. The production schedule (an Excel file)
2. The warehouse's inventory database (an Access database)
3. The work order database (an Access database which the production department uses to track incoming work orders from the sales department)
4. Microsoft Outlook (for receiving emails from the sales department)
5. The shipping system

6. The sales department's CRM system (for tracking customer sales information, including order specifications)

Application ID. Once the IT applications are inventoried, Matt and Kyle assign each one an Application ID. Since Kyle is the IT manager, he comes up with how IT Application IDs are assigned.[24] He decides to assign Excel spreadsheets the designation *IT-A-##*, Access database files *IT-B-##*, Outlook-related files as *IT-C-##*, and company-developed systems as *IT-D-##*. After doing so, they produce Figure 4-1.

FIGURE 4-1

Application Inventory

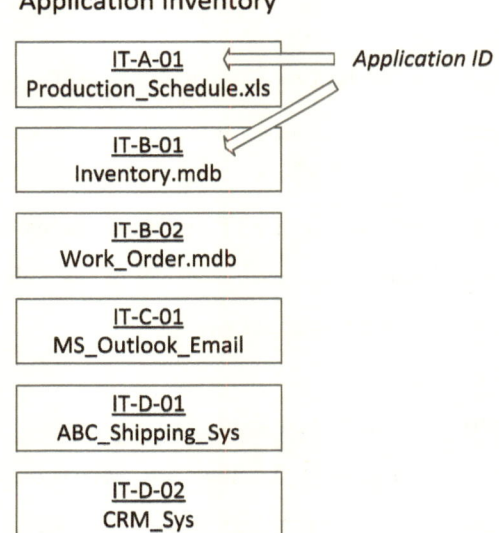

---

[24] Again, the exact classification isn't as important as having a standard. Your company may be an IT development company and so have a very complex ID system. Whatever the case, it should suit your company and be universal throughout the company.

60

With the appropriate Application IDs, Matt and Kyle now return to Figure 3-6 and draw the lines from the SOPs to their currently referenced Application IDs, as shown in Figure 4-2.

FIGURE 4-2

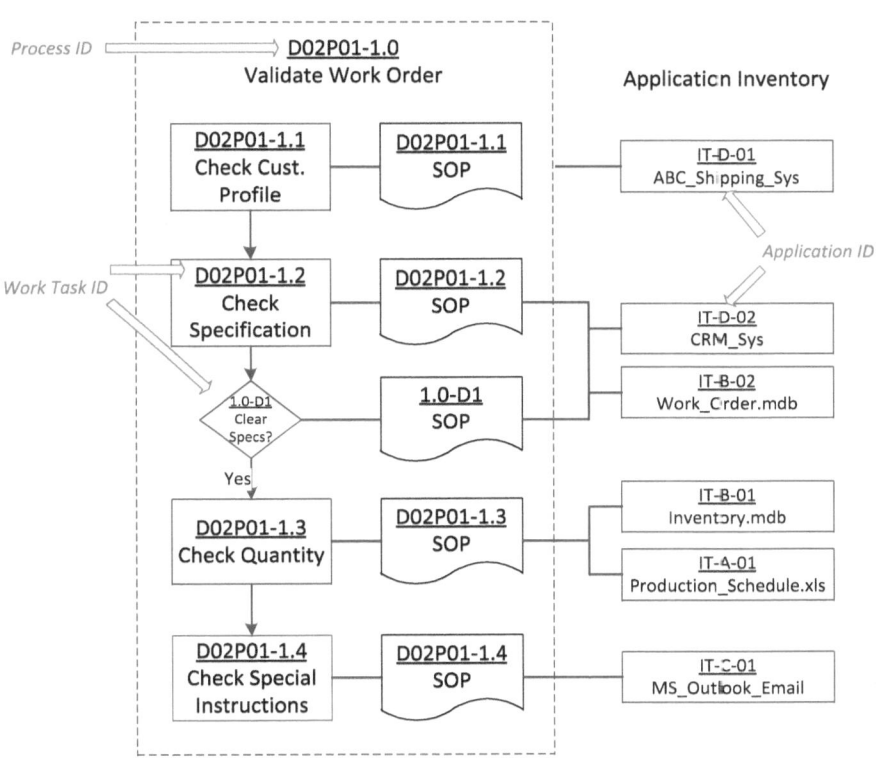

In the SOPs, the directions are detailed for carrying out each specific task, along with what application(s) to use, the business rules, etc. In addition to that, Application IDs are linked to their respective SOP IDs.

The flexibility of the PPT Framework is such that if the company implements a company-wide application for accounting, sales, marketing, finance, production, warehousing, etc., the processes Matt and Kyle have laid out will not change. To make the PPT Framework reflect the changes, they would simply update the related SOPs and reference new IT applications. The rest of the diagrams they have created *would remain exactly the same* (as long as the logic of the processes themselves remained unchanged).

One of the dangers of technology is that it is tempting for managers to distance themselves from the internal workings (the work processes, tasks, and decision/business rules) of their own department. Relying on technology instead of understanding all the tasks that are being performed can lead to managers simply becoming *users* of the system as opposed to architects of the work system. In this role, they are no longer catalysts for change and improvement – they are simply babysitters for the technology. In a worse-case scenario, they rely on technical experts as the catalysts of change (in which the technology often changes more than process improvements), running the risk of implementing a solution which does more harm than good. Also, automation and adoption of technology has a major risk often overlooked by operation managers. Having a core application which the entire department runs on creates a single point of failure; if the application is down, the whole department is down. Furthermore, depending on the importance of the department, politics, and the relationship between the operation manager and the IT manager, the core application of a certain department may not be a priority when the entire system fails.[25]

Seeing how well the PPT Framework addressed Matt's issue, Kyle considers applying the methodology to his own department, but

---

[25] Let's face it – as an IT manager myself, if a failure occurred that took out both the inventory system and email, and if the CEO lives and breathes by his/her email, then the inventory system will wait.

immediately feels overwhelmed. By taking just a quick inventory of the primary components of the company's IT infrastructure, Kyle comes up with Figure 4-3.

FIGURE 4-3

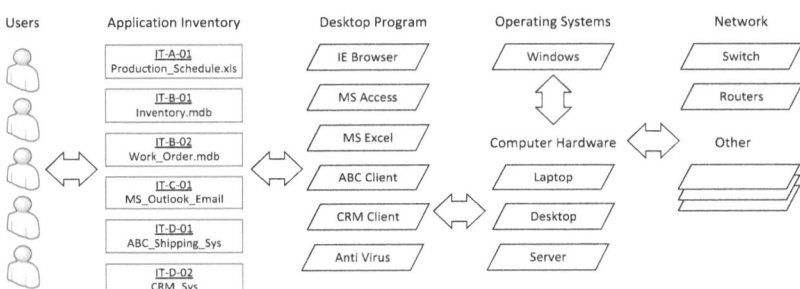

However, after thinking it through, Kyle realizes that his department does not *function* any different than Matt's. Like Matt, Kyle has a measurable output as a key performance indicator. While Matt's performance is measured in how quickly his department fulfills a customer order, Kyle's performance is measured in how quickly it takes to address an IT ticket or help desk request. Also similar to Matt's situation, the specific IT applications and hardware do not matter. Regardless of how technology changes, Kyle's staff is still responsible for maintaining IT resources and supporting the rest of the company on IT-related issues.

From a user's perspective, simply double-clicking on an icon opens the application needed to accomplish a work task. However, to deliver that icon and ensure it performs what it is designed to do, there are many hidden moving parts. This behind-the-scenes complexity is usually invisible to the users; it is the responsibility of the IT department to "make it happen."

As Figure 4-3 illustrates, there are many components that must be integrated together to seamlessly provide the desired solution. The complexity of IT management is that many of the components are developed and provided by various vendors, and more often than not the components' stability and compatibility with each other are outside the control of IT staff. Any component failure may render one or all of the applications unusable until the root of the failure is identified and corrected. Furthermore, as quickly as technology is advancing, vendors continuously provide revisions, upgrades, and rebuilds of their products. A change within any of these components may impact compatibility with another component, thus making upgrades a time-consuming and labor-intensive effort and virtually impossible to identify the business impact of the upgrades ahead of time.

A good example is when Microsoft decides to upgrade Internet Explorer with a major change in how the browser works. All applications programmed to depend on the older browser as the user interface have to be retested, fixed, and/or rewritten by IT to keep pace with the vendor and ensure each user application still functions.

I was involved in a project of migrating an organization with thousands of employees from Internet Explorer (IE) Browser version 6 to version 8.0. It required months to test and update dozens of web applications for the new browser version. Just a month or so after the migration of all the applications and employees, Microsoft released IE 9.0. Even while the company was publicizing that new release, I saw test versions for IE 10 announced by Microsoft. The same complication exists when Microsoft is moving from Windows Vista to Windows 7, or from Office 2003 to Office 2007 and then to Office 2010, etc.

A benefit of the PPT Framework is being able to quantify – in dollars – the value of a proposed technical solution, upgrade, etc. For instance, if Matt proposed automating the task of checking the quantity of material on hand[26], he could determine how much this would save his department by the following formula.

> (Time required to perform Work Task manually)
>
> **x** (number of times task is performed by a staff person)
>
> **x** (number of staff performing the task)
>
> **x** (hourly wage)
>
> = cost per period of performing task manually

If Mike, on average, took ten minutes to check the quantity on hand for the material needed for an order; if there were, on average, five orders per day; and if Mike's wage was $30 per hour, then:

> 10 minutes to perform task
>
> **x** 1,250 orders/year [5 orders/day **x** 5 days/week **x** 50 work weeks/year]
>
> **x** 1 person performing task
>
> **x** $0.50 per minute [$30/hour]
>
> = $6,250 per year

Thus, Matt can clearly demonstrate the value of automating this task if he made a budget request for an application. Moreover, Kyle could review the SOP associated with the task and understand exactly what the

---

[26] Work Task D02P01-1.3; see Figure 3-5.

application needed to do; all the business rules, criteria, inputs,. and outputs are clearly defined.

On the other hand, if Kyle proposed upgrading the CRM application to a new version, he could quickly see how many people would need to be retrained by pulling up the artifact documenting how many positions were linked to the SOPs that the application was part of. More importantly, Kyle could clearly show Emily and Matt how upgrading the CRM would benefit their departments by pointing out how each process flow, process, and task would be affected. Even though these three managers are from three different backgrounds – sales, production, and IT – they could perfectly understand what was being proposed and *exactly* what the IT upgrade would do for them. More importantly, Matt and Emily will have full ownership, control, and a decision-making role in when and where to adopt IT throughout the operational processes with full comprehension of its business value and benefit.

Here, at the end of Chapter Four, Matt and Kyle have resolved the short-term issue presented in the Introduction. After applying the PPT Framework step-by-step, Matt and Kyle have not only solved their immediate problem but have set in place a structure which can be expanded to include the rest of the company's processes in the future.

While the PPT Framework has the flexibility to change with the dynamics of the company, the marketplace, etc., it must be maintained in order to remain current and sustain its value. Applying the framework necessarily includes setting a governance process in place. Matt and Kyle address governance in Chapter Five.

CHAPTER 5

GOVERNANCE

Whenever someone comes up with an idea to solve a business problem, I congratulate them on developing their solution and then immediately ask, "How will we ensure this solution remains in place and provides ongoing value over time?" In other words, how will the solution be maintained so it becomes the standard way of addressing the issue instead of just a point-in-time solution?

The process of managing other processes, of operating in a consistent way, of adhering to company guidelines and principles, and clearly defining how the process of managing is approached is collectively known as *governance*.

Governance is extremely important in ensuring the system is responsive to the required changes while at the same time ensuring the integrity of the system itself.

Governance is critical for the long-term success of the PPT Framework. The idea of a systematic approach to managing people, processes, and technology is central to the methodology – including a systematic approach to managing the PPT Framework itself. Otherwise, the framework becomes another quick-fix solution in an array of haphazard approaches in a manager's toolkit – exactly the problem the methodology aims to eliminate.

There are four elements of governance in the PPT Framework:

1. People governance – ensuring individuals' skill sets remain aligned with their respective position, and their position remains aligned with its tasked responsibilities
2. Process governance – ensuring the documented processes of the PPT Framework reflect the on-the-ground reality
3. Technology governance – ensuring IT maintains a representative inventory of IT applications and iteration of upgrades, with appropriate documentation
4. Artifact governance – ensuring the PPT Framework itself is maintained, including all of the artifacts associated with it

People governance. Matt and Kyle developed job descriptions for each of the positions in Matt's department and also inventoried the skills of each of the people currently in each position. Because Matt made staff development a priority even before implementing the PPT Framework, nearly everyone in the production department is well-trained and well-matched to their responsibilities, so the skill development plans (see Chapter Two) are minimal.

However, Matt realizes that, with the pace of change in business and technology, having an annual performance review is simply too long. So much can change in just the course of a year – major projects forgotten, personal issues can arise, etc.; within two years, someone could finish a master's degree and be completely mismatched to a position. Waiting an entire year to review a person's accomplishments or take corrective action with deficiencies is ineffective. He decides to adhere to the PPT Framework's suggestion of a quarterly performance review.

Having a quick review every three months will allow Matt to:

- Ensure the position's job description aligns with reality
- Ensure the documented PPT Framework reflects what the position is responsible for
- Ensure the person is still aligned with the position
- Track how well the person is adhering to their skill development plan
- Facilitate communication and develop a better one-on-one relationship with each of his staff

With a quarterly performance review policy in his department, Matt feels he has a systematic approach in place to continuously improve his department overall.

While Matt and Kyle hope that HR will eventually take the governance of the PPT Framework on as their responsibility, they are moving forward with applying the methodology in their departments regardless. As Matt and Kyle move forward with the implementation of the PPT Framework, they realize they are potentially laying the groundwork for a company-wide adoption (if, as they suspect, it proves successful in their own departments). Even though it may be early for it, the two managers create policies and procedures for requesting, adding, and/or changing Position Titles, Position IDs, and job descriptions/required skills.

In addition, they index the relationships of the artifacts, as shown in the following table, which allows them to maintain the relationships between Departments, Position Titles, Position Numbers, Report-To's, and Employees.

Table 5-1

Dept ID	Position Title	Position Number	Report To	Employee ID
Dept01	Sales Manager	D01-00-01	President	###-##-#### (Emily)
Dept01	Sales Representative	D01-01-01	D01-00-01	###-##-#### (Tom)
Dept01	Sales Representative	D01-01-02	D01-00-01	###-##-#### (Jack)
Dept01	Sales Representative	D01-01-03	D01-00-01	###-##-#### (Susan)
Dept01	Sales Assistant	D01-02-01	D01-00-01	###-##-#### (Vacant)
Dept02	...	...	...	...
Dept03	...	...	...	...
...	...	...	...	...

Because each department handles their own budget, hires, backfilling of a vacated position, etc, the company's traditional org chart of chain-of-command has little value to operations. However, through indexing the people relationships by IDs developed in the framework, Matt and Kyle now have a relational view of people in the work system, as well as the ability to show the organizational hierarchy if needed. One example of using this index is the ability to see all the employees that occupy the same position title, so if a job description is to be changed, it provides an immediate view of who should be notified and retrained.

Process governance. After having documented the processes in the production department well and creating detailed SOPs, Matt and Kyle decide departmental processes should only be reviewed once per year. This annual review is similar to a retailer who takes inventory of their store once per year to rebalance what is on the shelves vs. what is in the books, and assesses the cause of the discrepancy. Also, the quarterly performance reviews touch the processes and work tasks throughout the department, which offers a secondary tool for reviewing processes.

Matt has considered creating a Production Planning Manager position and promoting Mary.[27] He decides that when he does, part of Mary's performance review will be how well she adheres to the PPT Framework for the production department. Since it will be Mary's responsibility to review the processes for the production planning functions (freeing Matt from doing so), Matt plans on performing periodic audits of different processes and work tasks to ensure adherence.

They also create an indexing table for process artifact governance which captures the relationships between all process-related artifact IDs as shown in Table 5-2.

---

[27] See Figure 3-5.

Table 5-2

Agreement	Origin Dept	Dest. Dept	Process Flow	Process	Work Task/SOP	Position Number
A01-02-01 (Work Order)	Dept01	Dept02	D02P01	D02P01-1.0	D02P01-1.1 (Check Cust. Profile)	D02-01-01 (Mary)
A01-02-01 (Work Order)	Dept01	Dept02	D02P01	D02P01-1.0	D02P01-1.1 (Check Cust. Profile)	D02-01-02 (Jason)
A01-02-01 (Work Order)	Dept01	Dept02	D02P01	D02P01-1.0	D02P01-1.2 (Check Specification)	D02-01-03 (Chris)
A01-02-01 (Work Order)	Dept01	Dept02	D02P01	D02P01-1.0	D02P01-1.2 (Check Specification)	D02-01-04 (Ken)
A01-02-01 (Work Order)	Dept01	Dept02	D02P01	D02P01-1.0	1.0-D1 (Clear Specs?)	D02-01-05 (Mike)
A01-02-01 (Work Order)	Dept01	Dept02	D02P01	D02P01-1.0	D02P01-1.3 (Check Quantity)	D02-01-05 (Mike)
A01-02-01 (Work Order)	Dept01	Dept02	D02P01	D02P01-1.0	D02P01-1.4 (Check Special Instructions)	D02-01-05 (Mike)
A01-02-01 (Work Order)	Dept01	Dept02	D02P01	D02P01-2.0	...	...
A01-02-01 (Work Order)	Dept01	Dept02	D02P01	D02P01-3.0	...	...
A01-02-01 (Work Order)	Dept01	Dept02	D02P01	D02P01-4.0	...	...
A02-03-1 (Ship Order)	Dept02	Dept03	D02P01	...	...	...
...	...	...	...	...	...	...

With the indexing of process artifacts, they are able to immediately identify all the Process Flows that may be impacted when an Agreement changes, the work tasks and SOPs impacted when a process changes, and the employees impacted when a SOP changes.

Technology governance. Technology governance is the only component of the PPT Framework which is assigned to a specific department: IT. Thus, it is Kyle's responsibility to keep a current inventory of all IT-related resources, including creating documents which outline the functions of each application and usage as it pertains to the company. Additionally, Kyle will keep an accurate record of which Application IDs link to which SOPs.[28]

Table 5-3

Work Task/SOP	Application
D02P01-1.1 (Check Cust. Profile)	IT-D-01 (ABC_Shipping_Sys)
D02P01-1.2 (Check Specification)	IT-D-02 (CRM_Sys)
D02P01-1.2 (Check Specification)	IT-B-02 (Work_Order.mdb)
1.0-D1 (Clear Specs?)	IT-D-02 (CRM_Sys)
D02P01-1.3 (Check Quantity)	IT-B-01 (Inventory.mdb)
D02P01-1.3 (Check Quantity)	IT-A-01 (Production_Schedule.xls)
D02P01-1.4 (Check Special Instructions)	IT-C-01 (MS_Outlook_Email)
...	...

This indexing allows Kyle to immediately identify the business impact when any application is not functioning, and managers can determine the contingency plans accordingly based on their mission-critical processes.

---

[28] For more information on managing IT, read about Information Technology Infrastructure Library (ITIL), Microsoft Operations Framework (MOF), or Information Technology Service Management (ITSM).

This is an important tool when planning for business continuity, disaster scenarios, etc.

For example, if the shipping system crashed and IT determined that it will not be recovered without a major rebuild of the server which will take two days, the warehouse manager should activate a contingency plan. The contingency plan may be to contact the carrier representative for alternate shipping information submission via fax, phone, or the carrier's web site.

For the purpose of this framework, IT is responsible for ensuring the inventory of applications is accurate. For each application, IT should develop a document which describes its attributes and associated policy of use.

These three tables (5-1, 5-2, and 5-3) represent the final link in the relationship of people, processes, and technology. They explicitly document how all three elements impact and relate to each other. They demonstrate how departments are linked, how information flows throughout the company, how technology is used, which positions are affected by changes in technology, and much more.

Artifact governance. Just in the limited application of the PPT Framework in which Matt and Kyle have engaged, they have produced a long list of artifacts – documents containing all the information related to the management of the people, processes, and technology Matt and Kyle have addressed. These documents include:

- The functional organizational chart
- Inventory of Position Titles
- Job descriptions for each Position Title
- Inventory of Position IDs
- Agreement Documents

- Process Flow diagrams
- Work Task diagrams
- SOPs
- File Repository Policy
- People Management Policy
- Process Management Policy
- Technology Management Policy
- Inventory of IT-related resources
- Inventory of personnel

Matt and Kyle realize that managing the artifacts related to the framework is a serious task, and will become even more so as they both expand the framework in their respective departments. In order to keep the framework standard across both departments, they see the need for a single repository of all the artifacts, as well as a single source for managing changes to the framework.

Ideally, the responsibility would fall to HR. However, since Matt and Kyle are implementing the framework independent of the rest of the company, they must decide among themselves who will be responsible for the framework. Kyle has more experience in documenting business systems as well as document management, so he volunteers for the responsibility (since he has extra time by *not* developing an application that Matt's department did not need to begin with).

Matt and Kyle create policies and procedures in regards to artifact governance as follows:

- Artifact creation tools, formats, and templates

- Procedure(s) for suggesting, evaluating, adding, editing, updating, approving, and/or removing artifacts
- Document version control

While artifact governance requires dedicated resources, such as staff time, the efficiencies gained from maintaining the framework will outweigh the costs in the long-term. The two managers now clearly see the PPT Management Framework is an investment – an investment of time and other resources which have a measurable return-on-investment for their respective departments and the overall company.

Matt and Kyle have now fully implemented the PPT Framework, even though they have only included primarily one department, one process, and one group of positions. They have solved a short-term problem which will add immediate value to the company and set the governance tools in place to ensure the process is well maintained.

After a few months, Matt and Kyle realize the framework is working so well that they decide to present it to the company in the hopes that it will be instituted company-wide. In the conclusion, they are asked to create a step-by-step guide to help their fellow managers implement the PPT Framework in their own departments.

CONCLUSION

After fully implementing the PPT Framework, Matt and Kyle became firm proponents of it. In the limited context they applied it, they decreased order fulfillment time by one to two days and contributed to increased productivity in the sales department as well. Unsurprisingly, when they presented their success to company leadership, the senior executives wanted to institute the PPT Framework across the entire company. The company owner requested that Matt and Kyle create an easy step-by-step document to support other managers in their adoption of the already-in-place framework. Knowing the value they are continuing to reap and the efficiency gains they have experienced, Matt and Kyle are eager to comply and create the following document for a generalized audience, along with some tips.

Preliminary. Obtain executive sponsorship and initiative buy-in, establish objectives and deliverables, allocate resource and time commitment, and develop structure and governance of work groups and committees. If you are implementing the framework on a company-wide level, executive sponsorship, buy-in, and commitment (or lack thereof) will ultimately determine your level of success. To obtain executive sponsorship, you must create a plan with objectives, scope, values, deliverables, and resource commitment clearly defined in the committee charter.

To avoid the initiative becoming a forum for department heads to launch turf wars, the structure of the initiative must be established prior to instituting the framework in terms of a chair person, facilitator, meeting format and documentation, members' expectations, and conduct.

Step 1: Identify the boxes (departmental entities) of the existing organizational chart or develop an organizational chart with upper management and counterparts. Give an ID to each department.

When developing the functional organizational chart, think strategically. The grouping should not be bound by your company's existing headcount or by considerations of *who* currently runs each department. The functional organizational chart should reflect the ideal of what the company structure *should* look like if it achieves its growth goals three to five years out. The functional organizational chart should represent the targeted state of an established and structured company. In smaller companies, this may mean assigning one person multiple roles (such as accounting and HR) due to the size of the business.

The idealized functional organizational chart sends a clear message of its ambition for growth to staff. It also identifies opportunities for staff to grow within the company, knowing that if the company achieves its five-year goal, manager positions will need to be filled. More importantly, it clearly identifies for managers handling dual roles that they must understand the two distinct functions they represent and make appropriate decisions for each without bias or preference.

Step 2: Assess company's mission, goals, and/or key advantages and establish a departmental mission that aligns to the company's. This mission should be documented, published, and communicated to/understood by staff, peers, and management.

Each department plays a role based on the company's key priority in terms of its market positioning against competitors. Knowing what that priority is provides a guideline for decision-making and priority-setting within the department.

A company president may feel that, in order to remain competitive, the company's priority may be to expand its market by developing new products, decrease order fulfillment time, increase production output capacity with new machinery or technology, all while adopting just-in-time practices and cutting total operational expenses by 10%. Achieving these multiple priority goals is unrealistic for a one year plan. However, tackling them as a five-year plan in phases, where each goal is the single priority for the year, may allow all of them to be achieved over time.

Step 3: You need to reach a consensus with your peers and executive management on a company-wide priority for the PPT Framework. This will be the single goal for all departments and managers across the company.

Allowing the owner or CEO to dictate which goal is the top priority may not be enough. All the managers from each function involved must buy-in to the priority. Each department is established for their distinct role, purpose, and skill that fit into the bigger picture. Depending on which priority is selected, there will be some disagreement between each manager's involvement, authority, work load, and benefit from the effort. This disparity can easily fuel conflict and hamper success if not dealt with early on.

Step 4: Determine entry (trigger) and exit points of the priority into and out of the company. Depending on the priority, this should be very straightforward. The trigger for the information flows between the departments must originate from somewhere external to the company. Also, if the established priority is truly a company goal, its end point will most likely be to an external entity, too.

Step 5: Map all the *existing* inter-departmental information flows, beginning with the external trigger and tracing the associated information flows throughout each department all the way to the final exit point.

A major source of mapping the inter-departmental information flows will likely be the forms[29] the company currently uses. As the managers draw lines between the department boxes, if a form exists in the company, name the line with the same name as the form. Otherwise, if departments hand-off information through automated processes or informally (ex. by phone or conversation), create a name for the line which best summarizes the information being passed.

When identifying the information flow lines, do not consider the method, medium, format, technology, and/or who is performing the communication. The only focus you should consider is the actual information being passed between the departments.

Step 6: Assess, evaluate, and agree upon the *ideal* information flow between the origin and destination of the identified information flows. Document and ID the new and changed information flows as an Agreement document between the managers.

For each of the existing information flows, form work groups or sub-committees involving the managers of the departments who originate each Agreement document and the managers of the department who receive the Agreement document. Carefully evaluate the information elements. The goal is to ensure the originating department provides everything to the

---

[29] For example, the work order form from Matt and Kyle's scenario.

destination department timely and accurately in order for the destination department to perform their processes with the incoming information as efficiently as possible with fewer exceptions from insufficient information.

This step is also an opportunity to eliminate extra information elements being passed to streamline the flow of information. It provides an opportunity to discuss various scenarios from experience that may be the exception to information flows between the departments. When scenarios begin to get complicated, adding to the required information in the Agreement document, ask, "How often does this happen?" If it is less than 20% of the time, exclude it.

In reading Matt and Kyle's scenario and the accompanying text, I hope you have discovered many of the PPT Framework's benefits and thought about how it could help your company or department:

- Engage in a systematic, scalable approach to continuous process improvement
- Set clear expectations and improve communication between diverse people and departments
- Create a valuable asset for operations, cost-benefit analysis, disaster/contingency planning, and business planning
- Implement a flexible, structured foundation for stable business growth
- Do more with less

In the current global economy, products and services are becoming commoditized. Companies have to consistently create high-quality deliverables at a competitive price just to be in the market – much less to thrive in it. I believe a key competitive advantage for businesses is, and will increasingly be, highly-efficient processes which clearly align people's skills with their responsibilities. By 2020, the *Wall Street Journal* predicts nearly one-fourth of people will be 'free agents' – contract workers who work on a project- or contingent-basis, rather than full-time employees. Now, more than ever, companies need a framework that allows for the kind of flexibility which addresses the new needs/demands of the workforce *and* the new needs/demands of the global marketplace.

I hope you agree with me that the People, Process, and Technology Management Framework is just that.

AUTHOR'S NOTE

This book is designed to be an introduction of a series of people, process, and technology management books I plan to develop and share with you. As you are aware, it is almost impossible to account for the various scenarios and challenges a company may face internally in wide array of industries. Thank you for taking the first step of seeking a solution and a methodology for addressing your specific management challenges by reading this book.

I, too, am a manager who seeks answers to management challenges, and I plan to continually refine and improve upon my techniques and framework as I find more answers. I welcome the opportunity to develop my future books through a collaborative approach with my readers by sharing scenarios, thoughts, and ideas at my website, www.kan-wang.com. Through periodic short publications, and through blogs and discussion topics on my site, I hope to help you apply the framework and find solutions to your unique challenges.

Lastly, as I start my next book project, *Principles of Analyzing Information Technology for Non-Technical Managers*, I welcome your input on the challenges you may be facing as a non-technical manager which you believe should be covered in the book.

ABOUT THE AUTHOR

Kan Wang has an MBA with concentration in management, an MSCS with concentration in computer information systems, and a BSc in business administration and economics with concentration in management information systems. Starting in the information technology field as a developer, he reached the level of upper management and executive management consultant working in industries as diverse as e-commerce, manufacturing, and government. His fifteen years of experience included positions held as both an IT manager and an operations manager, and from a unique perspective from both sides of the table, he witnessed hundreds of scenarios where the disconnect between business and IT limited a company's efficiency and growth. The author is currently an information technology Officer at the Riverside County Department of Public Social Service, and also a lecturer with the University of California Riverside A. Gary Anderson Graduate School of Management.

ACKNOWLEDGEMENTS

To my daughter, Emily, and my son, Ethan: you were the inspiration for writing this book. The two of you coming into my life changed my perspective on the purpose and value of my existence. You've taught me success is not just defined through what I am able to achieve in my career, but what I can help others achieve. More importantly, you've made me think about what kind of world I can leave behind for both of you.

To my wife, Lisa: you've always been there for me through the ups and downs of life and supported me every step of the way. From my pursuit of business and career ventures to my education and dream of making a difference in society, I know you will always be behind me with words of encouragement and endless love and support.

To my parents, Cathy and William, and my sister, Helen: thank you for sacrificing your careers and dreams so I can pursue mine here in the United States. Further, thank you for taking care of Emily, Ethan, and Lisa by providing a loving and caring family atmosphere for them as I pursue my dreams.

To Dr. Robert Kwortnik, thank you for your class and lab hours fifteen years ago which challenged me to live up to your example as a great teacher and an inspiration to others. I hope I can be to others what you were to me. To Dr. Stanley Abraham, Dr. Joyce Kupsh, Richard Kung, Paul Cheng, and Chi-Sun Chang, thank you for your support and confidence in my ability to teach and educate others.

To my friends Robert and Amy: thank you for the quiet workspace you provided in your company as I wrote this book.

Kan Wang

www.ingramcontent.com/pod-product-compliance
Lightning Source LLC
Chambersburg PA
CBHW022111170526
45157CB00004B/1581